The Commando Entrepreneur

Enjoy!

Damian.

The
Commando
ENTREPRENEUR

Risk, Innovation and Creating Success

Damian McKinney

URBANE
Publications

First published in Great Britain in 2015
by Urbane Publications Ltd
Suite 3, Brown Europe House, 33/34 Gleamingwood Drive,
Chatham, Kent ME5 8RZ

A CIP catalogue record for this book is available
from the British Library.

ISBN 978-1-909273-61-0
EPUB 978-1-909273-62-7

Design and Typeset by The Invisible Man
Cover design by Julie Martin

Printed in Great Britain
by CPI Group (UK) Ltd,
Croydon, CR0 4YY

urbanepublications.com

The publisher supports the Forest Stewardship Council® (FSC®), the
leadinginternational forest-certification organisation. This book is made
from acid-free paper from an FSC®-certified provider. FSC is the only
forest-certification scheme supported by the leading environmental
organisations, including Greenpeace.

"To all the veterans, who gave selflessly,
we owe so much"

Contents

The Commando Entrepreneur

Testimonials

"Outstanding people are no mistake. Built by an extraordinary psychology, they push progress by seeing more clearly, learning more deeply, and acting more decisively than the crowd. Commandos don't dabble. They decide. They deploy. They deliver."

Alex Pratt, Founder of Serious and author of 'Austerity Business'

"Damian and his team brought their Commando Way and high-performing teams approach to us during a transformative time for our company. The work they've done with my leadership team and me has greatly influenced the way we communicate with each other and work together. During a time of challenge and change, we maintained a unified focus on our end goal while driving a new strategic approach throughout the organization. We exceeded our stretch plan while we performed as we transformed during the largest restructure in company history. What we learned from McKinney Rogers kept us on target, on task and in line with what we set out to accomplish."

Stu Crum, Chairman and President, Bridgestone Retail Operations

"This book is a must-have if you are working through how to deliver break through results for your firm. A clear strategy is important, however, the execution of that strategy with a well selected team who are supported with the correct type of training is key. Without this it is not possible to sustain the changes necessary to drive businesses on."

Howard Boville, Managing Director, Technology Infrastructure Bank of America

"One of Africa's greatest, Nelson Mandela, said that it always seems impossible until it is done. This strikes resonance with a special breed of business people who Damian has referred to as Commando Entrepreneurs. What I believe this book does is that it equips these special breed with the mind-set and tools to execute the pursuit of the near impossible, and the means to mobilise disciples in charting a path where none existed before."

Austin Okere, Founder, CWG Plc & Entrepreneur in Residence CBS, New York.

"Management is process oriented, really successful leaders are visionary, but entrepreneurs work and discover in the unknown. Damian marries this convincingly with military commandos who operate behind enemy lines are disciplined and yet react and disrupt. A truly unique perspective."

Neville Isdell, former Chairman of the Board and Chief Executive Officer of the Coca-Cola Company

Acknowledgements

I am not an author in the true sense of the word, but one who regards it as an ideal opportunity to share ideas that I have experienced first-hand, which I believe can really make a difference to people's lives and the organizations they support. Hopefully reading this book will motivate you to take up the challenges, to believe it is possible to achieve the impossible. The journey through life I have experienced from childhood is what has inspired me.

I attribute this back to my early childhood growing up in Kenya, my time in the Royal Marines where I learned so much about leadership and motivation and the amazing business experiences I have had since. It is with this in mind that I set out to write this book. I believe that there are numerous crossovers between the military and business. At a time when we have so many veterans entering the corporate world, I am compelled to encourage everyone to look at these servicemen and women as the amazing individuals they are, who have grown up very quickly and will make a huge difference to future organizations.

All of this work would not have been possible without the continued support of a number of very special people: my exceptionally supportive and loving family, especially my mother Liza; wife Krissi; and children Charlotte, Alex, Flora, Sophia and Benjamin - who all continue to inspire every aspect of my life. My many mentors over the years from: "Mr. Chitty", my first headmaster at the Banda School who took a risk and made me captain of the first XI Cricket team when I was thirteen; to Peter Williams and Graham Cooper, my rugby coach and housemasters' respectively at Kelly College, who gave me the belief and confidence at school that I must always aim for number one, anything less was disappointing; to General Robin Ross; Brigadiers Allan Hooper and Graham Dunlop; and the many Royal Marines and other members of the military, who trusted me at a very young age to take the lead and 'have a go.' Together with my Commando training, they taught me the real meaning of giving people belief and confidence in themselves. This set me up for life.

I also wish to thank those special people who have mentored and stood solidly by me during my business journey, through both challenging and great times, in particular Steve Wilson, Martin Akers, John Esposito, Bill Simon, David Haines, Andy Fennel, John Nicholson, Gerald Mahinda; Claire McCarthy, Lisa Davis, Jin Iwamoto, Chris Stephenson; Orlanda Atherley, Will Casselton and the team at McKinney Rogers. And not forgetting John Simmons for his tireless support and patience supporting me with this book.

Finally, to the many real friends who are the true commandos in my life. They are the ones who always stood tall and never ran!

Damian

Foreword

A year ago I would have laughed at the prospect of introducing a book about 'commando entrepreneurs'. I would have been baffled, perhaps a little uncomfortable with the military connotations. But now it seems natural and I am happy to do it.

What has changed is that I met Damian McKinney, the author of this book, and through that experience I learnt that my stereotypical reactions were wrong. I still find the military a little baffling but I now understand what someone like Damian, with his commando background, brings to the modern corporate environment. I sum it up as a mixture of clarity and mental agility.

That mental clarity was needed when I talked to him, somewhat skeptically, about working with our leadership team at Health First. Damian came to us by recommendation. Here was I, a female chief executive of a growing not-for-profit healthcare organisation with 900,000 members in New York and an extremely diverse staff. I challenged Damian: with your British Royal Marine background, can you talk to such a diverse audience, can you make a real connection with them?

I need not have worried. Damian has many qualities – boundless energy, intuitive understanding of people, an ability to listen and then to go straight to the heart of the matter. He is a sharp assessor of people's strengths and can quickly suggest the roles that they can play best. There is a flexibility in his approach but it is given strength by the structure of his thinking.

As a Royal Marine, Damian was trained to think. This book will give you countless examples that you can usefully apply to your own life and business. His message is much more subtle, much more tuned to diversity, than my preconceptions had first allowed. The more I got to know him, the more I recognised his ability to understand individuals and, by doing so, to get the most out of teams.

That is important. Damian's ideal commando entrepreneur is a team player not a lone wolf. Within the dynamics of a team, bringing together people of many kinds, he knows the importance of a clear mission if the team is to function to its full potential.

In this book Damian sets out the characteristics of a commando entrepreneur. These come from his instincts for people, knowing what makes people perform at their best. The characteristics are ones that we can all understand, but there is also a subtlety about them that I find attractive. This is not a black and white view of the world.

I relate to that. We all work in a world that is constantly changing. What succeeded yesterday might not succeed today. We no longer have such certainty about what is good, bad or indifferent – we certainly know that it is different.

The working world is now increasingly virtual. You may never see or meet many of the colleagues you work with. This puts even greater emphasis on the need to be absolutely clear and to work within the parameters of the mission. The mission is a beacon. It's a beacon whose importance was instilled in Damian by his training.

He carries it now into his business practice and into the ideas expressed in this book. It contains a message that I believe has a particular resonance for the future as well as the present.

We can no longer take security from past success, we have to keep learning, proving and improving ourselves every day. Because everything in the business landscape is changing so fast we need to be more mentally agile than ever, and we need to keep our minds open to new possibilities. I have learnt that Marines have that quality. When I came across the US Marines' motto – Adapt, Innovate, Overcome – it resonated with me and with my team.

For me as a woman running a large organisation, whose people fully reflect the diversity of the world in terms of gender, ethnicity and background, I welcome the different perspective that Damian brings. It's not helpful for CEO's to talk only to others who are just like themselves. I value the fact that Damian's background is unlike mine in just about every way imaginable.

What matters to us as human beings are the essential qualities we hold in common, the qualities that we admire and learn from. So, if we share a belief in mental agility, emotional intelligence and a drive to succeed, this is a book for you. I suspect you are a commando entrepreneur in the making.

Pat Wang, CEO, Health First

Chapter 1

The need in uncertain times

In my previous book **The Commando Way** I set out the context in which businesses have been operating: a context of uncertainty. We have to acknowledge that times have been tough. In fact, in the three years since that book was written times have, if anything, got even tougher. The situation has even gained its own acronym – VUCA standing for volatile, uncertain, complex and ambiguous.

The strategic shocks I described then continue to reverberate across the world. The first of these was 9/11 and we live in a world that still feels the repercussions from that event.

This was followed by the second strategic shock of the 2008 financial crisis. This changed the financial environment overnight and the world's economies are still adjusting to its aftermath. Few of those economies are operating as buoyantly as they were before the crisis, and the expectations for growth remain relatively restrained. This remains a challenge for businessmen and women around the world.

Adding to that fragility is the situation that I pointed out as potentially a third strategic shock, the turmoil affecting the Arab nations in particular. We simply do not know what will be the long-term effects of the uncertain political, military and economic situation of the Middle East.

I wrote then that "Uncertainty is now the norm". This inevitably affects the philosophy with which we conduct business. A shifting commercial landscape leads to the need for new rule books and behaviours. The old command-and-control business model is obsolete, and businesses need a new model that encourages individual initiative, leading to business execution that is faster, more creative and more effective.

Otherwise the old-style businesses, too slow-footed and late to react, get left behind and spin into a cycle of decline.

For people working inside corporations this age of uncertainty can lead to risk-aversion and a lack of motivation. Employees become less and less clear about their company's direction and objectives, and therefore less clear about their own role in achieving success. Trust and enthusiasm leach out of the business and leadership teams become dysfunctional. People feel less valued and less engaged.

On the other hand, spurred by technological changes, we all now have greater abilities to exert influence on a volatile business environment. The ways of communicating, gaining knowledge and using that knowledge to good effect, have multiplied with the increasing understanding and enhanced methods brought by digital technology. Potentially it makes us all quicker, more flexible, better equipped to anticipate and respond to changing environments.

How best to respond?

My proposal was, and it remains, that there are certain people better equipped to respond to uncertain situations because of their training, experience and natural inclination. Of course, I draw on my own knowledge of both the business and the military worlds. I see many similarities between the two, but we need to set aside any stereotyped preconceptions about military behaviour. I am not advocating the charge of the Light Brigade. Indeed, faced with similar situations in a modern setting, trained commandos would today take a very different approach from the headlong, full-frontal assault. Commandos are trained to think and come up with solutions that work. Those commandos - women as well as men – know that mental agility is more important than physical strength.

The approach I set out in *The Commando Way* is based on the idea of mission command, adapted from military expertise to the world of business. It's a model that's proven and that adapts well to these uncertain times.

In the business environment we need to adopt principles of mission leadership. The central principle is that a mission has a **what** and a **why** but does not specify **how**. Teams and individuals are therefore crystal clear about what they have to do (their own mission) and why (how it aligns to the overall mission). This provides clear freedoms and constraints, and encourages teams to develop solutions that are driven by those individuals who lead teams informed by a clarity of objectives and a sense of purpose.

My argument – based on countless examples from my own involvement in the business world – is that these principles are instilled into every commando and they transfer easily into the business environment. There are obvious links too to those people in the business world who are called entrepreneurs. In fact, so close are they in spirit and attitude that I now call them commando entrepreneurs. It's a concept that this book explores in much more detail, drawing on examples from my own experience of working with such people in corporations and organisations across many different countries.

It's important to stress that not everyone I call a commando entrepreneur has been on the receiving end of military training.

These are people marked out by the necessary characteristics but who might never have been near an assault course. The characteristics needed relate primarily to flexibility of mind rather than physicality of body. For example, one person I would cite as a commando entrepreneur is Angela Ahrendts, former CEO of Burberry. She invited me to work with her leadership team because she could relate to the principles I set out here.

When Tim Cook, CEO of Apple, recruited her to be Senior Vice-President in charge of retail and online stores, he created the dual role especially for her. He believed that she could achieve Apple's mission of serving customers better because of her particular qualities and embrace of Apple's values. As he put it: "She believes in enriching the lives of others and is wicked smart". That statement provides a good first marker for what I mean by a commando entrepreneur.

Technology, as Apple demonstrates, is one enabler but people at work now have different mindsets about what is important in life. The way we think about our careers is very different from, say, thirty years ago when I and my peers were first contemplating career paths. We give more thought now to purpose and it is no longer seen as hopelessly idealistic to want to make a difference. This opens up the range of career possibilities as well as the opportunities for getting more out of each job. This mindset – constantly seeking to get more out of a situation, to go further, to stretch beyond comfort zones – is one that commando entrepreneurs share.

The role of a commando entrepreneur

In any business, but especially in challenging times, there is a need to be clear about your purpose. Mission leadership demands it while emphasizing the value of teamwork that comes from aligning everyone behind that purpose. This empowers people to think for themselves about how they can achieve that clearly defined purpose for the business – and for their own personal satisfaction to align the individual and the corporate purpose. It does not require detailed instructions on what to do but concentrates on building the simplest possible understanding of why the business aims to do it. In effect it releases the entrepreneurial instinct while keeping within the framework of commando principles. That's why it's liberating. And it's also why it works. It harnesses instinctive, imaginative power within a tight sense of discipline. The concept of freedom within boundaries is one to which I will return.

Importantly it leads to extraordinary performance. It provides a way to integrate the individualistic into the collective, the maverick into the corporate, enabling a small selected cadre of business commandos to operate to maximum effectiveness, as in the military. This cadre can achieve challenging objectives that drive a business to faster growth and higher targets. These commando entrepreneurs are pathfinders who create the conditions for others to sweep in and exploit success. The ripples of their actions spread outwards rather than trickling down from the top through traditional hierarchical structures. The approach leads to higher performing companies that achieve their missions.

Not everyone is a natural commando entrepreneur so there is a skill in identifying who has the right qualities to be one.

The aim of this book is to make it easier for you to spot such individuals. You are seeking people to take on the toughest breakthrough tasks, requiring entrepreneurial skills of risk and innovation. Risk does not mean gambling; it requires accountability. No commando ever wishes to jeopardise the success of the mission by taking unnecessary risks. So you need people who pay close attention to detail.

As with *The Commando Way* principles, the starting point is the business's values that need to become personal and real. Never compromise the DNA of the business but recognise that very few have the particular DNA to become a commando entrepreneur. You need to be absolutely clear about the end state you aim for and the value that achieving it will bring. Then stick to it. Because successful businesses need leaders not just managers.

Leaders set the tone and the environment within an organisation and this empowers the commando entrepreneurs to flourish. They also enable the same characteristics to develop more strongly in those who are not natural commandos or entrepreneurs. In doing so they notch up the overall performance of the organisation to a higher level than would otherwise be achieved.

Crossing the bridge

Finally, for this introduction, let me ask you to think about this through the example of a military mission that succeeded to extraordinary effect. It involves a bridge, but it also creates a bridge for you to think about how these two – the military and the business worlds, supposedly so different - are in many respects alike. It is an example that many of us have been reminded about in recent times. June 2014 was a time to commemorate the 70th anniversary of the D-Day landings that were so vital in speeding the end of the Second World War.

In 1944 the war had already lasted five years. The Allied forces, under the strategic command of the American General Eisenhower, were at last gaining the initiative in Europe. The end state of an Allied victory could now be imagined, and General Eisenhower set out the mission of defeating the Nazis in mainland Europe.

Forces assembled secretly from many different countries, and with the hands-on involvement of the British Prime Minister Winston Churchill in the planning, the D-Day landings brought into action hundreds of thousands of soldiers. Beaches in Normandy on the northern coast of France were identified as places where the large numbers of troops would land. Boats were readied in English ports and harbours to carry the troops and equipment to mount the attack. The German army was well-equipped and battle-hardened; they had controlled France for years and were deployed into defensive positions against any military invasion from England. It was clear that any battle would be hard fought and that victory could not be certain. But these would be the decisive actions of the war.

To succeed the Allied forces needed to surprise the Germans. Secrecy was vital. Even if the initial landings were successful, Eisenhower knew that the Germans would respond quickly and with great force. So he needed to limit the speed and power of that response. To achieve this objective, he needed a small group of airborne commandos to play a decisive role.

In the early hours of 5th June 1944, a force of just 181 men took off from an RAF airfield in southern England. They flew in six Horsa gliders. Gliders were used because they made no noise and could maintain surprise; but they were also much more difficult to fly with accuracy and with a glider there could be no return flight. The generals in command decided that it was a risk that had to be taken, and the small British glider force was clear and determined to achieve their mission. As well as courage and a refusal to be daunted by risk, the troops involved needed to display mental agility because there was no way of knowing what conditions would face them on the ground.

The mission was to capture two bridges inland near the coast of Normandy and to prevent German armour from crossing those bridges. If the bridges remained under German control, the counter-attack on the landing troops would be overpowering, leading to higher casualties and jeopardising the success of the overall mission.

Under the command of Major John Howard, five of the gliders landed as close as 50 yards from the target at 16 minutes past midnight. The small band of Allied attackers poured out of the gliders and, aided by the element of surprise, overwhelmed the German troops defending the bridges. The action took ten minutes; two brave airborne commandos died in the short battle.

The sixth glider landed some seven miles away. The soldiers disembarked and moved through German lines until they rejoined the British forces. On the same night these expeditionary troops, who now controlled the bridges, were reinforced by men from the 7th Parachute Battalion. These combined forces then linked up with the army landing on the

Normandy beaches, including commandos led by Lord Lovat.

Lovat's team, No. 1 Commando Brigade, was crucial to the D-Day success, maintaining the speed, surprise and flexibility that was essential and preventing German counter-attacks. Lovat famously landed in the first landing vessel on Sword Beach with the skirl of a piper playing alongside him. Secrecy was no longer needed; the action was under way. But the success of that action depended to a large extent on the commando behaviour of the men who captured and held the two bridges after landing by glider.

Seventy years later, surviving members of the D-Day landings gathered at what is now named Pegasus Bridge (after the parachute insignia of the airborne commandos). They gathered in the now peaceful village of Bénouville. A moving ceremony commemorated the role of the soldiers who had done so much to achieve victory for the Allied forces.

What we learn

For me this is a powerful story. I find it powerful because it is true and because of the courage and selflessness shown by all those who took part. It shows brilliant teamwork by the commandos and by those who acted like commandos and by all the other participants. Many people, playing different roles, combined to lend their efforts to achieve the same overall mission. I'm interested in the role played by the small dedicated cadres within the whole and I wonder whether victory would have been gained as swiftly and effectively without them playing this role.

I also find the story powerful because there are lessons that can be learnt from it, and those lessons can be applied to businesses operating today. This is a story of brilliant strategy and extraordinary execution. These were made possible by an absolute clarity of mission, by the skill, boldness and imagination of a small group of motivated people, and by the trust placed in that group. That is something from which every modern business can learn.

The Commando Entrepreneur

Chapter 2

What makes a commando entrepreneur?

Commando. Entrepreneur. In one sense this is a tricky combination of words. Each word is capable of being easily misunderstood. The phrase 'commando entrepreneur' came to me from my observation of many people in the business world who were called entrepreneurs, but who seemed to me to have the qualities and values of commandos. They were resolute in their pursuit of excellence; they were not daunted by the size or difficulty of a challenge, indeed they welcomed it; they never gave up, they remained positive in all circumstances; they were absolutely clear about their values and their mission.

It was a simple step to turn this around and think what qualities a commando might share with an entrepreneur. Again there seemed a close match. Commandos have to operate like entrepreneurs. They are never daunted by risk, they have a sense of adventure that keeps them positive, they are confident in their ability and their role to make a difference, and they constantly strive to achieve what others regard as difficult if not impossible.

Perhaps too they enjoy the challenge of finding their own way. They enjoy arriving at a solution that achieves the mission in their own way rather than simply heading off down the obvious, well-trodden path.

Commando/Entrepreneur. Entrepreneur/Commando. Are they interchangeable? Do they share a common meaning? No, because each word adds an extra dimension, another layer of meaning to the other, and those layers come from the mingling of influence from their military and commercial origins. A commando entrepreneur is different from someone who is a commando or an entrepreneur. At the same time the commando entrepreneur comes in many different forms. He or she is not made from an identikit of parts that make them easy to spot.

Defining a commando entrepreneur

Inevitably we need to start with each word. What do we mean by 'commando'? It is a word that can be seen through a distorting lens of romanticism or prejudice. While 'entrepreneur' has become a buzzword leading to a fuzziness of meaning, a faddish word that gets loosely applied to an enthusiastic business person. For me both words are more specific, so let's start with 'commando'.

In *The Commando Way* I set out the values that easily transfer from the Royal Marines to the way I have always run my own business. These are values we live by at McKinney Rogers, values familiar to Royal Marines and that make a commando:

- *Pursuit of excellence* – Be the best you can be.
- *Courage and determination* – Never give up.
- *Humility and humour* – Be gracious and honourable.
- *Cheerfulness in adversity* – Maintain a positive attitude.
- *No sense of class* – Be inclusive, diverse and positive.

If those are values that define a commando, I believe they are also values that an entrepreneur will recognise and relate to. I regard an entrepreneur as a seeker of ideas, someone able to think ahead into the future. This does not mean a state of being perpetually curious for the sake of satisfying curiosity. An entrepreneur seeks ideas that will fix seemingly intractable situations. When something is not working as it should be ('something' might be a business) it needs fixing. There is a thrill gained from fixing a problem that in the perception of others seems extremely difficult.

These are also characteristics that a commando will recognise. You cannot be an entrepreneur and afraid of losing money, just as you cannot be a commando and worried that the weather might take a turn for the worse. So the commando entrepreneur combines the closely related values of both mindsets.

A commando entrepreneur sees 'impossible' as a challenge not a deterrent. The risk of failure is not a problem, it is simply part of what they embrace in life and work. At the same time there is no rigid distinction between life and work for commando entrepreneurs. There is no striving for work-life balance, their life is their work, it is what defines them. As Angela Ahrendts of Burberry and Apple said about her work:

"I've never considered it work. It's a natural extension of my life."

The reward for the commando entrepreneur is not primarily financial. The main motivation is being able to make a difference. When you solve a problem, and you make a difference in doing so, people smile. That is the reward. In the Royal Marines very few people get medals; they do not seek them. You simply do what is expected of you – and that gives you the excitement that is a large part of the entrepreneur's attitude, to aim for excitement rather than to win medals.

This is not thrill seeking, but it does mean a love of the adrenaline that comes from being set a mission and trying to deliver it.

In pursuit of that mission, the commando entrepreneur needs to display doggedness, just the sheer force of will to find a solution and get something done even though – or especially because – people say you cannot. You do not give up, you keep on because you believe you will find the answer.

The answer is there. You just have to find it. The commando entrepreneur's attitude is to find a wire that will make a connection rather than to seek millions of dollars to make something more easily achievable.

That is an attitude that becomes drilled into a commando in training. Otherwise you will find it impossible to operate for much of the time. You find yourself, for example, in the Caribbean at a time of fuel shortages, with little equipment and hardly any money. The answer, for the commando in that position, is not to say "let's wait for the situation to improve" but to head for the market, buy rice and bullets and then set out on your mission. Because you have been told that this mission is vital. You are committed to the mission so you find a way to pursue it.

In pursuing it, the commando and the entrepreneur share a common approach that goes beyond the normal, the average. They share a determination to find a way.

There will be risks in doing that but there is a misconception about the approach to risk. The commando and the entrepreneur take similar approaches to risk-taking – neither is ever reckless. If you are gung-ho about risk you will not survive for long. You are willing to take personal risks but you are committed to the success of yourself and the team. If you are reckless you endanger the team. The phrase instilled in me (originally from my grandfather) is:

Bring all your people back alive – it is your job to look after your people.

We should not confuse entrepreneurs with investors in entrepreneurs. Entrepreneurs are the commandos who go outside the den to deliver the mission – it is their drive and ingenuity that will win the day. Cash is the fuel that can help drive them. But entrepreneurial investors are business people who trade and make transactions, measuring their success by financial returns. The return for the commando entrepreneur is not measured first by the amount of money earned – the return is assessed in terms of the adventure, the excitement that comes with success. It's a different way of assessing risk and return.

When I joined the Royal Marines, I was sent to collect my pay at the end of the month. That was when I discovered how much (or how little) I was being paid. But already I was being rewarded with adventure. Not everyone loves adventure. There is a Darwinian selection process based on aversion to risk: "No, you can't do that". The negative command is a challenge to the commando entrepreneur, almost an invitation to find a different way to achieve the same end.

In the corporate world a couple of years of "No, you can't" can lead to conformity. But successful businesses thrive if they can work with not against the non-conformist. The high performing companies will encourage entrepreneurs within the business rather than drive them warily outside.

Not every entrepreneur – inside or outside a corporation – succeeds every time. Not every commando achieves his mission every time. But I believe that commando entrepreneurs achieve more because they attempt to do more. Inevitably they sometimes fail. But when they fail, they bounce back.

Some businesses worry about this, and questions loom. Do we need to accord privileged status to these people? Will we need to pay them big bonuses? I am not convinced that this is so – the stake is the second layer of motivation. The first layer is not about money but about adventure. If the motivation was just about money, behaviour would be contained and constrained by money. This would not be the behaviour of a commando entrepreneur.

In a business context, the encouragement and integration of commando entrepreneurs is about co-existence. As in the military, not everyone is or wants to be a commando. The saying goes that 99.9% of people need not apply to be a Royal Marine or a Commando. So, in the corporate environment, there are a small number of people with the real inclination to be an entrepreneur. But these are people who will be lost to the business if they are not recognized, nurtured and encouraged. And, if they are lost, there is the possibility that a significantly higher level of performance is lost with them.

We have to enable the commando entrepreneur to co-exist within the business alongside those who have different personalities and motivations. How do you blow oxygen into them so that they perform more brightly for the benefit of the business?

There is a folk tale in the Caribbean about crabs in a bucket. The crabs share that bucket and there is little chance of a way out. But one crab will always try. Usually that crab is pulled back by the others. Perhaps that is why we use the word crabby about mean-spirited behaviour?

I suggest that healthy businesses will want determined individuals to rise to the top. There should be no pulling back down to mediocrity. Mediocrity achieves nothing. We need to understand that, in any business, different people are equipped to play different roles.

Commando entrepreneurs take the role of creating the conditions for others to exploit. This might involve invention, product development, breaking into new markets. Areas that make a real difference.

This means you cannot have complete loners. The commando entrepreneur is not necessarily happy when given a solitary mission – he thrives on teamwork. *The Commando Way* set out the importance of *everyone* in a business being signed up to the same rules of engagement: to share values, to focus on the vision, to be aligned to the mission, to foster team spirit. The true commando entrepreneur will not be an oddball maverick with no interest outside self-centred ambitions. He or she will understand the conditions that will enable success.

These qualities are instilled in a commando in training and operations. But not all commandos are Royal Marines, and not all commandos are men. A military background is not a requirement. I have worked with and admired many people in business who received not a single minute of commando training yet display all the essential qualities of a commando entrepreneur. Similarly, in the business world a commando entrepreneur can be a woman – indeed there need to be more women in that role as Steve Wilson states later in this chapter. It is the mental and behavioural characteristics that are crucial to the definition of a commando entrepreneur.

If I use analogies from my own military background, that is

the experience that I can draw on. And I draw on it to make points about the business world that I also know well. In Iraq I learnt that it matters where you pitch the first tent because in a short time that tent will lead to the growth of a town. With large numbers of refugees arriving, I ordered the first tent to be erected, which was then followed by many more. When inspecting that first street, seeing that a small initial error became larger tent by tent that was erected, I knew that I had to make the marines start again. When the second through to the fiftieth tent form a street, details matter, they exaggerate the overall picture. Small details become multiplied into a big problem. Six inches out of line grow to yards and miles when 50,000 refugees need to occupy the space that you are filling.

On the other hand, I am not a boot camp believer. I am not one to obsess about polishing brass buttons. What matters is the pursuit of excellence, and my belief in that pursuit is very high. I believe in pushing standards, in hitting targets. "What's the fastest it's ever been done?" Let's try to do it faster.

I listened to Roger Bannister, the world's first four-minute miler, on the radio recently. Now in his eighties, he was recalling that historic run on the 60th anniversary of setting the world record. Did you do it for yourself or your country? he was asked. His answer was "For both". Like a commando entrepreneur he had a mission and he was determined to achieve it, fuelled by the chance of making a difference. We all respond to a clear mission, but we particularly need commando entrepreneurs as driving forces to achieve the mission.

It is about quality and standards. In business, in the military and in other areas of life, you are associated with a badge, a brand. Anything less than full commitment to the highest standards lets down the badge – so you aim high, you succeed or, sometimes, you fail. If you do not aim for those standards you fail, but you have no excuse.

Commando entrepreneurs aim for those highest standards. Succeed or not, they need no excuse because their own standards are the highest. So is a commando entrepreneur born or made? As always in life, it helps if you naturally embrace the values needed, but there is always more that can be done to enhance those qualities and abilities through training. The training I received from the Royal Marines is something I still draw on now, and still use in my work with companies of all kinds. Later in this book I will explore what are the aspects of that training that can help to make a commando entrepreneur.

But it will help at this point to give you a real example of someone I think of as a commando entrepreneur, someone I have worked with in the business world over the last decade.

Portrait of a commando entrepreneur

Steve Wilson comes complete with many years of experience in the drinks business with major companies and brands. I regard him as a true commando entrepreneur though he looks at me slightly askance when I say so. That is just Steve: he is absolutely straight, slightly cynical, without a trace of self-glorification. He just wants to do the best he can and will never get carried away by his own achievements.

The reality is, he has achieved a great deal. I first came across him at Diageo, the global drinks company that had been formed in 1997 by a merger between Grand Metropolitan and Guinness companies. I had been brought in to coach the Global Brand executive tasked with turning Johnnie Walker round. Steve was head of Global Innovation after the merger and I first met him one day at the coffee machine. It was just a chance meeting but a fortunate one for me.

Steve was a key player in the integration team for the newly created Diageo company. He had soon discovered that a merger is trickier than an acquisition. His task was to integrate two marketing teams and make them one. But there were two different cultures, two different sets of expectations; two ways of operating, with two groups of people who had equal power and were jockeying for position.

The challenge was all to do with people and behaviour. Steve had been given project management support but systems would not solve the problems of getting people to work together as a team. After we'd talked for a minute or two while drinking our coffee, Steve asked me "Do you know anything about team building?"

It was, as he admitted, a slightly naive question but it led to a good conversation. We agreed to meet again and soon we were working together on what became the model for High Performing Teams, which remains one of McKinney Rogers' core products.

Together we put all the people of the Diageo global marketing team through the programme. It worked well, and we got to know each other well. Steve wanted to make things happen, which meant encouraging everyone to reach out and help each other, to cast aside any parochial thinking. He also got the leadership team to take responsibility for the result not their result. In effect he followed the Commando Way, with everyone clear about their team and individual missions.

Steve has some military background but he is not a marine. He won an RAF scholarship as a young man but it did not work out as he thought it might. He took a sabbatical from the RAF to work at a drinks company where he soon decided he had found his career. However, while working full-time he joined the RAF Air Reserve. That continued for 22 years but he never went back to the military as his career. Steve continues his story:

> "Being in the military, even to that extent, gave me a comprehension of what military life and training is about. The public perception is that it's like the Wild West with all guns blazing. That's a long way from the truth. If you serve in the military for 95% of the time you are in training. There is a commitment to training that has stuck with me. You are trained to get things done, with the least fuss."

> "This was brought home to me again recently when I was involved in a charity venture. As part of this I spent three days on a warship, HMS Montrose, in the Mediterranean. The ship had a company of 130. Everyone knew their job, knew exactly what they had to do, and the whole operation was seamless and painless. The captain, with all this responsibility, was 26 years old. The crew were younger and everyone had been well selected, trained and rehearsed for every eventuality. This was the principle of Operational Rehearsal in action."

The question of selection exercises Steve. He believes it is a big difference between the military and the commercial world. Businesses need to learn to do the simple things better, and that starts with selecting the right people for a role. Steve explains it like this:

"Companies need to think harder about how they recruit people. They mainly assess the qualifications that applicants have. Are you qualified to do a certain role? They look at your degree, educational achievements, certificates, but they don't really evaluate aptitude. Then they move people around and promote them until they reach a level of incompetence. It's the Peter Principle. It's not that the person is an idiot, just that he or she has not been prepared. What do you want this person to do?"

"The military does that well. It takes more time and effort to select and then it gives much more attention to deeper training. It's a big step that companies have to take. If companies really want to make a difference, they have to think more about what kind of people will make a difference. These are people that you call Commando Entrepreneurs."

That is a good description. I believe it is important to have people working with you who really want to make a difference. Most companies have them but might not have identified them in a rigorous way. Leaders tend to know who they are: these are the people they trust and go to for special tasks. They need to be spotted, nurtured and encouraged but there might be more of them in a company than you imagine.

If there are not enough in your company, you have to hire people who will carry out the roles you want in the business. Steve stresses that people cannot do everything. If you want the best company in the world, you have to think about people with the best skills to deliver what you need. And they need to be able to bring the best out of others who work with them.

"It's often a case of teasing out who these people

are," continues Steve. "Which individuals can make a difference? Take a look at who you've got and who you might need to hire. Invest in recruiting and training them."

"Back in the 1970s, when I was starting out, there was much more emphasis on training. Originally I was a chemist by training, and that put me in a quality control role in the first drinks company I joined. Then I moved into R&D, then I was put onto a special project – a bit like a commando entrepreneur, I suppose, given a mission to lead the way into new territory. One special project led to a succession of special projects. One of them was the creation of a new product and brand, Bailey's Irish Cream. It did well. There were many others."

*"It is about having a mission, being very clear about what you need to achieve. The military does that well. It's not about blindly following orders. I've never minded being told **what** to do but I prefer to take my own approach to **how** I do it. The people who are commando entrepreneurs love the clarity of a mission and they love being empowered to deliver it."*

Steve and I agree that the military are good at selecting and deselecting people. If you do not make the grade you are told so clearly. If you do make the grade you are given every encouragement to keep developing. If you are a marine commando you are selected for tasks that are more challenging. In Steve's case I recognise his special abilities: he is brilliant at creating and fixing brands. At first this was in the drinks industry but he discovered that the same questions apply in other businesses too. So what are those qualities? What does Steve think are the qualities of an entrepreneur?

"There's a mistaken vision of the entrepreneur as someone who makes stuff happen by being cavalier and breaking all the rules. To be honest, definitions of an entrepreneur along those lines are too loose. My definition is that, yes, the entrepreneur makes things happen inside a business. To do that he or she needs ability not authority – this might not be the person with 'leader' in the job title. What that person needs, above all else, is interpersonal skills. By using those skills entrepreneurs in a business bring people on board, create effective teams and consistently deliver."

"They make a difference, and that makes them commando entrepreneurs. They have a skills set, and in time they acquire experience. The alignment means you can take on the most difficult challenges that make a difference to an organisation. Can I fix that? Yes, of course I can. The fundamentals are the same in any organisation. But the bigger the organisation, the bigger the supertanker and the greater the problem in turning it round. Even more in that situation you need people who can spot what they need to do; the greater the need for cut-through."

"It's different from leadership. Companies define leadership by function. The functional leader need not be – often is not – a commando entrepreneur. Businesses don't define what they want a leader to do. That 'leader' almost certainly needs people who can make a difference at great pace and consistency. The leader and the commando entrepreneur can be the same person but the problem is relatively few people have the necessary qualities."

Pressed to describe those qualities, Steve puts these forward:

- Action orientation. An ability to roll up sleeves, take a hands-on approach to solving a problem.

- Good at teamwork. Showing the ability to support and coach, giving others opportunities to succeed and protecting them from fear of failure.

- Motivated by success. Results matter more than money because results will lead to money, money will not always lead to results. Success, not money, provides the motivation.

- Good with people. An emphasis on the need for personal skills, which includes being a good communicator. The ability to get along with people and to bring people along is vital – being able to do so socially matters.

Steve recalls his recent experience with the captain on *HMS Montrose*. When the ship was leaving harbour, the captain invited Steve up on to the bridge. A 22-year-old was in charge of piloting the ship out, a tricky task in a narrow stretch of water. He carried out his task with the captain sitting in the high chair, observing, saying nothing. After the manoeuvre was completed, when the ship was safely out of the harbour, the captain spent ten minutes giving the junior officer high quality feedback, positive and negative. Not an end-year performance appraisal but advice that will stick and lead to higher performance.

The military is predominantly a male organisation but Steve does not believe such skills apply only to male-dominated businesses. Far from it. his theory is that women have more highly developed interpersonal skills because they have had to develop them to survive and prosper. Women make good commando entrepreneurs for that reason. Because it is generally tougher for women in business, they have to work harder at relationships and the interpersonal skills that will bring out the best in others. They find ways to bring people on board.

The question of risk is central to the subject too. Steve draws on his experience to emphasise that businesses need people prepared to take risks but not at any cost. The important thing is to understand what the risk is and to manage it. If a project has a high probability of failure, fail small. If there is a low probability of failure you can risk more. Companies have to profile risk. No one should risk bringing the company down. Test small so you can fail small.

It is good advice. Steve backs it up with an example from a time early in his career when he was launching a product – at the last minute they discovered a labelling problem. Should the stock be withdrawn? The advice came "We can afford £1000". A simple measure; every company will have equivalent measures by which to assess risk. But no company will want cavalier risk-takers. Each company needs to assess its appetite for risk-taking. When you take a decision, you have to know what the risk is. The cavalier 'entrepreneur' is not good at calculating risk – the commando entrepreneur is.

Businesses need to give the freedom to fail; which becomes the freedom to succeed. If people get fired every time they fail, your business will never succeed.

Again Steve backs this up with his own experience. When developing a white rum brand to compete with Bacardi, he failed miserably. The company lost £25 million. Steve got a call from the CEO to see him in his office on a Friday afternoon. "How are you doing?" the CEO asked. "I guess you want to fire me," Steve replied. "But why would I do that? I've invested £25 million in you. I want to know what you have learnt and what you will do next time as a result."

Military debriefs have a similar purpose. We can all fail but we all need to learn from failure. We need to manage the size of the risk, and we need to give people the environment to succeed without being constrained by fear of failure.

* * *

Through this pen portrait of Steve Wilson you are beginning to build up a picture of a commando entrepreneur. But of course there is not a single mould that produces them all. Commando entrepreneurs represent diversity.

Are there, however, common qualities that define them? I believe there are, and in the following chapters I'll set out what those qualities are, using real people as examples.

Chapter 3

Never daunted by risk

In the next four chapters I will explore the characteristics that I believe make a commando entrepreneur. There are different routes to that particular designation but a true commando entrepreneur will have each of these characteristics to a greater or lesser extent. The first of these characteristics, discussed in this chapter, is 'Never daunted by risk'. Each characteristic relates to the others, but there might not be an even spread – not 25% each. The variation might come from a person's background and, of course, natural personality - and it might be shaped by following one of these three routes:

- Someone trained in the military to become a commando who later became a successful entrepreneur.

- A corporate leader, possibly but not necessarily with a military background, who has both the commando and the entrepreneur in outlook and execution.

- An instinctive entrepreneur, with no military association, who has the DNA of a commando, displaying values that relate to those of a commando.

Whichever route is taken in a career, the commando entrepreneur will have a particular attitude to risk. The question of risk is an inevitable one in business and, for me, it is crucial in creating the grounds for business success. Because you cannot succeed in business without taking risks; and you will fail in business if you are foolhardy in taking risks. The commando entrepreneur exercises judgement in assessing risk, understands its importance and will always seriously weigh up the pros and cons of any particular action.

This process of deliberation, which might be almost instantaneous at times, is never a reason for prevarication. Decisions have to be taken, and these lead to actions.

Commando entrepreneurs are more than usually conscious of the need for action, and are always aware of the risks involved. But they are never daunted by risk. That characteristic – never daunted by risk – is the first clear characteristic of commando entrepreneurs.

They are not daunted by risk because they generally see the risk involved in any action, project or enterprise as an opportunity to achieve something remarkable, rather than as an obstacle demanding pause and inaction.

Risk comes from not knowing what you are doing but that can be helped by training. That's why commando training is so rigorous (which I'll return to in Chapter 8) and it's where businesses need to improve and learn. Risk also comes from not knowing what you are trying to do, and this risk can be more or less eliminated by following the principles of the Commando Way that focus on establishing clarity of mission.

It should be said too that commandos – and commando entrepreneurs – are survivors. They recognise when the odds are too heavily stacked against them. They know when it might be best to find their way around an obstacle.

There are rules that companies follow in relation to risk. Martin Davis, as a leader of a multi-billion financial services company, will talk about that later in this chapter. Those rules need to be taken seriously but commando entrepreneurs do not follow them slavishly. For example, in Walmart – a company I know well from working with them extensively – they have a number of company rules that they expect people to follow. But the final rule is:

"Break all the rules"

There is a commando entrepreneur spirit in that, something I have observed and felt in Walmart. It is not about encouraging anarchy, simply saying that the people might need to think more unconventionally to achieve the company's objectives within its ethical framework.

Not every risk-taker is a breaker of rules. Not every entrepreneur is a maverick unable to function in a corporate system. Many entrepreneurs – Guy Hands, for example, who set up Terra Firma – state the advantages of the support given by an organisation combined with the freedom to express yourself.

There are, of course, costs that come from taking the risk of action, but perhaps they are not as great as the risks of not taking action or taking it too late. Business is a matter of choices and decisions. Clearly there is a 'gap' between the businessperson who is risk-averse and the commando entrepreneur who has a higher risk tolerance. But in reality, it is not a gap that separates safety from its opposite. Commando entrepreneurs always calculate risk and they work out ways to mitigate it – in the long run the commando entrepreneur's approach is based on the chances of succeeding rather than of failing. Interestingly, the commando entrepreneur with the bias to risk mitigation can often reduce the 'gap' to less than that of the business person. However, the real knockout blow is that the commando entrepreneur continues to 'what if' planning when executing, which further reduces risk of failure. Thus a risk-averse approach, ironically, might be at greater risk of failing because excessive caution leads to inaction.

I do not think it is true to say that entrepreneurs have no fear of failure. It is just a matter of how you assess the risk, and an entrepreneur (like a commando) might feel that there is a natural risk in life. Perhaps that risk is even welcomed because it gives a bit of a buzz and these are people who love adventure. The fear of failure is always there but it is there as a threat to ego rather than fear of conventional threats like the loss of a job or money.

Let me illustrate some of these points by setting out the results of an interview with someone I regard as a good example of the commando entrepreneur.

An interview with Martin Davis

Martin Davis is Chief Executive of Kames Capital, a £60 billion investment company based in Edinburgh. He has military training ("land-based," he smiles, "not a marine"). Actually Martin's service was distinguished, ten years in total, including two tours with the special forces. After the second of these, following the Gulf War, he studied for an MBA then went to work at Reuters.

That is where we first met. I was there to help Reuters deliver their strategy more effectively. Martin, because of his military background, was volunteered to use his team as guinea pigs. We worked well together; so well that we stayed in touch and Martin in time played two roles for McKinney Rogers. First, he stepped in as part-time managing director for a year. Later he became a non-executive director until his work commitments became too heavy. At that time he was selling his financial services company Co-funds, a business he had grown substantially.

From that short description you might easily understand why I think of him as a commando entrepreneur, a title he finds 'intriguing'. Now no longer connected to McKinney Rogers he remains a believer in the company's philosophy.

> *"I'm always concerned,"* he says, *"about the disjoint between strategy and execution. I see it everywhere in companies. Senior management is often disconnected from the guys on the ground floor. It's an important issue that business leaders need to face honestly. I've been able to do that effectively with the help of McKinney Rogers in several situations."*

Martin has managed big businesses in financial services including Zurich and his current leadership role at Kames (which was previously Aegon, and a long while ago Scottish Equitable). I am sure his own experience of military command has made him more aware than most of the potential and actual disconnect between people at the top and the front line, between strategy and execution. He expressed it to me like this:

> *"What are the qualities shared by the two – the military leader and the business leader? I see these qualities applying to both. There's a focus on high performance, and the constant wish to make a rapid response. You have to keep your head up, looking around, while constantly moving."*

> *"I see that in the military, but I value it even more in business. The word 'entrepreneur' conjures up a Dragon's Den image of someone with a personally-driven idea, starting a business from scratch, seeking a big injection of money to get that business off the ground. I'm less interested in that kind than in what we might call 'corporate entrepreneurs'. These are people within large organisations who work in an entrepreneurial way."*

"I think it's this second group who are the commando entrepreneurs. They're distinguished by a clarity of purpose. They are also highly resilient, totally committed to getting a job done."

"When I look at leadership generally, I see the need for and the value of emotional resilience. There's a determination to carry on despite all the pitfalls along the way. Many leaders unfortunately lack this resilience but it is there in the commando entrepreneurs. I look for those entrepreneurial qualities in people in my business."

"Of course, it's never absolutely clear-cut. I think there is even a sub-division between those who need a crystal clear direction to be set for them and those who enjoy a greater flexibility."

"For example, if you have identified the goal you wish to achieve, you need to find the right person to do it. This will not necessarily be the toughest and ugliest who will smash his way through towards the target. You need someone to navigate through the business, to stay nimble, but keep the end-point in mind. You look for a self-starter who has resilience to get on with it and find ways around obstacles. There's a risk, of course, that you get the wrong person and you have to clear up the trail of destruction."

"That's why I make the distinction because I think the most interesting commando entrepreneur is not always sure what the best route to the mission is. Of course you give him or her a mission. However, there may be options in how you achieve that mission. Perhaps options A, B and C are all possible and they all improve the situation. But which is the best? It's a problem-solving creative

approach, and there are different tasks that suit different people."

"Perhaps the first person is going to launch a great product to a defined market and the second is going to explore what is the need and therefore what is the product going to be. Either way, something needs to be done, and something gets done."

"I think of the situation in my career where I was starting and growing a business in the world of internet banking – in those days before internet banking existed. We were winning customers in Australia, Malaysia and Greece from bases in the UK. We had to tweak for local requirements out of the US, still winning deals while developing the business model."

"We had to build local service models that leveraged the international model we knew best. Someone was needed who could assimilate a lot of information quickly while foreseeing what the market would be like twelve months ahead. There is an art in focusing on what can be delivered, the ability to come up with a plan, then do it. All this in the dotcom period when a week was a long time ahead."

"The person who did this job for us came up with an answer that was unexpected. We had given him a broad brief and his solution of two service centres, with a hub and a spoke, was not what we had envisaged. It was right for the time. We trusted him."

"In the military, the mission is as tight as possible to ensure success. The focused mission succeeds: take that hill rather than take the western flank. Often in business

your mission needs to remain as tight as possible while allowing for the possibility of other approaches. This requires an individual with a different skill set – this is the commando entrepreneur."

"If I give a broad brief, trusting a highly talented individual to perform a task, my expectations are not that he will come back to my office in two years' time and say "job done". The broader the mission the greater the range of options, the greater the need for communication, so you need someone who is a communicator. It's a lot to do with ego – that person does not want to fail, he does not want to look foolish. So he needs to feel comfortable with coming back at any time to check things out. On the other hand, I don't want someone knocking on my door every ten minutes and saying, in effect, look how clever I am'."

"So you want someone willing to come back, to test ideas, to understand what you have to do. That takes confidence actually, it takes an ego. You have to strike a balance."

"Take the example of Andy McNab's (Bravo Two Zero) mission; he's someone I knew and with whom I worked. Four people were given that same mission. One decided it was impossible and never set out. Two others got there but aborted the mission because the terrain and weather were so much against them. Andy cracked on. He knows he should not have continued but he did and he succeeded. It was about ego."

Whether his stories are from the business or military worlds, Martin is aware of the need to assess risk and act upon that assessment. The more you are used to assessing risk, the less you are daunted by it. In his current role, with £60 billion of funds under management, the financial risks are mind-boggling. So I ask him how his approach to risk differs from the financial business to the armed forces.

"In the military you can argue about whether a mission was achieved. There will be different opinions: did we succeed in Iraq? But it seems to me that the difference between success and failure is clearer in the financial world. In finance, it is completely transparent. Let's say we aim for a cash return plus 5%. It's going to be very clear whether you have failed or succeeded. There's a number – you hit it or you don't."

"This transparency means that the risk element is greater because failure is clearer. So at Kames we look at everything in 15 different ways. It's a complex world of risk, much more process-driven, less instinctive, more rigorous in setting numerical targets than the military. Because of that transparency, the target for success is also clearer, and this means that people still want to take risks. They simply have a better idea of what the risks are."

"Where it all becomes similar to the military is when the planning is done. As in a battle, you have a plan, but no plan survives the first encounter. You have to react. Something happens, you respond, risk management is in play. We have systems that decide to risk no further, to cut the life support systems off. There's a risk blanket to remove danger but of course failure is always possible – look at UBS, Barings."

"Fundamentally it's still all about human behaviours and we all react differently. That's why businesses seek those

individuals who can make a difference. Look at the fund managers, they know that the past is no guarantee of the future. They have more information than you can shake a stick at but they have to be decisive and fast. People buy you."

"The fund managers chase their 5-star ratings. There is interesting evidence to show that the performance of 5-star fund managers drops off 80% after three years. It's a matter of psychology. When you chase the five stars you are happy to take risks to make gains. Having got there you are not happy to take risks to make losses. Your attitude to risk changes once you have something to lose."

* * *

Martin is a commando entrepreneur operating at a high level in the financial world. His risks revolve mainly around money. I next wanted to get the perspective of someone who has been financially successful but has achieved success by taking different kinds of risk. This goes to the heart of what business and governments need from security.

An interview with Damian Perl

Damian Perl is extraordinary. He trained as a Royal Marines officer but resigned his commission early. He then joined Special Forces not as an officer but as an ordinary trooper. He has an instinct to do things but he remains a careful thinker. I would describe him as a genuinely creative person, brilliant at finding lateral solutions to problems. He never planned to stay long in military service but it was an adventure for his 20s;

he would see about the future later. Each of those sentences reveals an individual attitude to risk.

So after his three years tour, he left Special Forces. He was nearly 30. In the military, Damian had never enjoyed the emphasis on structure and was to an extent different by age, education and background from a number of his peers. On something of a whim, as he puts it, he joined a large British security company – a well-trodden path at a relatively easy level for many who come out of military service. Damian found aspects of the work interesting, much of it routine, and he was not impressed with the way people were treated nor with how customer relationships were developed. "There was little imagination in the role."

This experience showed him that there could be a better way. Damian always looks for better ways. He took on more roles for no more pay but much more interest, gaining more central coordination roles, dealing with logistics and liaising with governments and other organisations. In short, he saw an opportunity to set up his own business that he named, with some chutzpah, Global Risk Strategies.

He was entering a market where, in the UK at that time, there were two big, established players. The people from these companies had connections into government, defence and other industries. It was a bit of a closed shop but Damian chose to compete with them although he had no money, no connections, no business knowledge. He set his business up in his spare room in south London. He bought a desk, he had a phone, he borrowed books from the local library on business and law. He taught himself about corporate and employment law, about balance sheets and branding. He designed his own website. Then he set about networking and cold-calling with real determination.

As he spoke to people, he aroused interest in what he could do, but he received reactions like: "Why would I hire you rather than companies with track records and many years of experience? I have to be accountable for my decision-making." All the risks were being taken by Damian (soon he was to take out his third re-mortgage of his flat) rather than by business corporations.

It was dispiriting but eventually he landed a contract to work in southern Africa. The contract demanded more of his brain than his brawn. After a couple of years, this security programme (for a bank) had provided money and credentials. Damian returned to the UK and took a small office in central London and hired two members of staff. More cold calling followed. He won a North Sea oil security project, and a few others. The business was up and running, enough to enable survival. It was hard graft and he was broke.

9/11 changed everything. It changed the dynamic in the security sector and Damian saw opportunities to help while growing his business. I describe more of this phase in a short case study later in the book, where the risks were to life and personal safety more than to business finance. Suddenly there were demands at new frontiers such as Afghanistan where few companies had recent experience, which created opportunities for a small, nimble, innovative company. Damian won work which was successful, profitable and opened new doors with businesses and governments globally.

By winning work for organisations including the United Nations (UN) and a number of Governments Damian increased his influence and was able to respond quickly to new business demands. Suddenly, what had seemed a risky venture a few years earlier, had grown into a substantial international business living up to its new name Global Strategies Group.

He further developed business particularly with the US Government, bringing into his team people with high-level connections in the defense and security sectors.

How had it happened? What made this possible? Damian made the following points.

"To be honest, in the early days, to some extent I was making up a lot of it as I went along. I'd go into a meeting and they'd ask 'Can you do this?' So I said 'Of course I can'. Once I got out of the meeting I asked myself 'How the hell am I going to do this?' but it was just the same in the military. You received an order 'Take that hill'. You never questioned the order but you did wonder 'How the hell am I going to take that hill?'"

"The thing is, we always got it done. The company became very good at finding a solution. I realised that everyone, in every business meeting, had problems. At that time, the person offering the innovative cost effective solution got the work. This was different from before where cosy relationships had often meant more than solutions. The situation and the problems in places like Afghanistan and, later, Iraq were new to everyone so relationships were less important than effective problem solving. I have to say the Government contracting environment for security services became far more prescriptive in later years but the company evolved its core offering and business practices beyond that and we now have a varied group of stakeholders where there's still the same need for smart innovative thinking."

"Many of my early actions and success came from that training I had. It taught me self-belief, determination, lateral thinking, comfort in trying the difficult – traits that

the Royal Marines recognise and inculcate in all recruits. They simply drew out of me what was already there. I must have had a natural resilience to get through difficult times, and part of that is not worrying too much about taking risks. At the same time I always look for a Plan B – fact is a Plan Z can be handy. But, since leaving, I've never missed the military – I left with a blank sheet, I could put on it whatever I chose, and I liked that."

Damian's is a worldwide business from the US to Europe the Middle East and Asia, and he is no stranger to 18 hour days and working on planes. It requires physical as well as mental endurance. The business was initially built on offering integrated security services to key Government and commercial clients around the world, but in recent years Damian has, in his words, elevated the business to being first and foremost an investor in and developer of critical national security technology, achieving two separate IPO of Group owned companies on the NASDAQ exchange and managing a range of private investments in mission critical leading edge capability.

"I'm proud of what we've done but I tend not to wave the flag. I prefer to let actions do the speaking. I believe that's another commando trait. I demand a lot of my colleagues but I try to set an example. Another commando trait is to learn and adapt. Nowadays as the business leader I focus on strategy, leading business growth and change, critical decision making and working with our key stakeholders, while delegating to my senior team the things that they do better than me."

"It's funny, when I think back to my Marines training, I looked around and thought 'everyone is so different'.

But there was something in common that had been identified through the selection process, and over time it becomes clearer. So when I meet up with that group of people or people with a shared or similar background we appear fundamentally the same, there aren't that many differences. The training brings out particular traits in you that were latent. But going into business added the dimension I needed. I never thought of it as a risk, just something I had to do."

* * *

I hope you are building a picture in a similar way. Damian and Martin are very different but united, I believe, by shared characteristics including 'never daunted by risk'. Inside each of us there is at the very least a recognition of these characteristics and a sense that we all would wish to share them. Damian is a special case, though, almost embodying "Who dares wins", the SAS motto. But we could all strive harder to welcome new challenges and not to be so afraid of the new and the unknown.

I will conclude this chapter with a short case study about an individual and a company that seemed to find each other and bond around a shared approach to personal and corporate risk-taking.

Case study

Heineken - Dolf van den Brink

Attending graduate fairs in the Netherlands, Dolf van den Brink looked destined for a career in finance. But he was never quite convinced it would be right for him – a little safe, perhaps? Dolf met a sales rep from Heineken who told him stories about the on-trade, dealing with bars, restaurants and, above all, people. Dolf decided to join Heineken: "I wanted to develop as a people manager".

He moved around, learning marketing, then was put in charge of a tiny part of Heineken's business in Holland, a small product, and he had one employee under his wing. Out of the blue he was asked to join Heineken's business in the Congo as commercial director. This would mean managing 700 people, all but two Congolese-born, in a part of Africa that had been troubled and where the language was French (he did not speak French).

For an outsider this seemed an intimidating challenge. His first thought was to say No. He had his wife to consider too. But visiting the country with his wife, she showed an adventurous spirit, saying she was 'in'. He accepted the job, knowing that his five predecessors had left the role in fairly quick succession; knowing too that in the World Bank Group's 'ease of doing business' rankings, Congo was just about bottom.

Dolf spent time travelling around unannounced and unrecognised to get a feel for the country. As he did so he learnt French. When he officially started he said to his boss that he had butterflies and received the reply: "Don't worry. You'll go under a couple of times and we'll pull you up by your hair."

At first he struggled. There was something in the African culture that involved formality and deference to rank; it did not suit him so he ditched the tie and jacket to follow his wife's advice:

"Just be yourself. Stop pretending."

He knew there were big problems in the market so he started small, focusing on one neighbourhood with 20 outlets.

Success at that small scale built confidence; people believed, he was given the nickname Papa Plus. The figures showed why. He reclaimed lost territory as Heineken's, one neighbourhood and one week at a time. It was a market that responded to an aggressive, entrepreneurial attitude – a thousand small things rather than one big idea. Heineken's market share grew from 31% to 75% in four years, driven by the value he adopted for the business, *esprit de corps*, fighting spirit. "It's mission leadership not command and control. You rely on the guys making choices, having their own autonomy in the field."

Next he was offered another big job – to be CEO of Heineken USA, the beacon market for Heineken globally. He has been doing that for four years and has had an energising effect on the business. It was another risk, on both sides. Would many companies have given the Congo job to someone with so little experience? Would many companies have offered the top Heineken USA job to someone whose main experience was in a commercial role in the Congo?

Risk-taking can work in two directions, as this case study shows. Dolf took great personal risks with his career and his family, and it paid off because he was not daunted by risk. But in many ways it was Heineken as a company that took the greater risk. They decided to send an untried young man to a challenging environment in the heart of Africa that was unknown to him, and then they took a further risk in promoting that still young man to run their business in the world's most important market, the USA.

Dolf says he learned leadership in the Congo, and added greater thoughtfulness in the USA. This was a person and a business that showed commando entrepreneur instincts.

Chapter 4

A love of adventure

The second characteristic I suggest for a commando entrepreneur is not seen in many business books. 'A love of adventure' might be a bit too romantic, a touch reckless, or perhaps it might sound too much like fun to be at ease in the serious corporate world. But as a Royal Marine I always believed in working hard and playing hard, and a love of adventure brings work and play closer together.

Obviously there is a relationship between the first characteristic discussed in the previous chapter and this second characteristic. 'Never daunted by risk' and 'A love of adventure' are linked. But it needs to be stressed, as with risk, that a commando's love of adventure is always accompanied by a weighing of possibilities. No true commando will thoughtlessly endanger himself or his colleagues for the thrill of adventure. There is always a time to know when to retreat, when to pass, when to refuse a challenge that cannot be won.

In Victorian times, the journalist and economist Walter Bagehot wrote the following:

"Adventure is the life of commerce but caution, I had almost said timidity, is the life of banking."

Perhaps in the light of 21st century economic history, we might not quite as readily associate banking with timidity, but it is interesting to read Bagehot's statement that adventure is the life of commerce. Not everyone 'in commerce' is fond of adventure, but I believe that every entrepreneur is. They enjoy the thrill of not knowing what awaits them on the next working day.

The love of adventure means that entrepreneurs enjoy trying to create their own destiny. It is a different mindset from the salaried employee who takes comfort from the security of repetitive and predictable tasks. It is about action but it is more importantly about thinking. In an adventure the lead player needs to think: to anticipate what might happen next and to think in reaction to what has happened. It is not about being fatalistic and blown wherever the wind takes you. 'Adventurers' try to control their own fate, enjoying the freedom that they gain by doing this.

But you need to seek adventures, rather than let them happen to you. Perhaps it is this active seeking of uncertainty that distinguishes and unites the entrepreneur and the commando. It makes life more interesting, it puts you on your mettle, and it is always good to be tested. As noted in my introduction, we live in times of great uncertainty, and in such times businesses need people who operate at their best in unpredictable situations. Businesses need people who can react well to the unexpected.

The adventures considered by this book are not of the Indiana Jones kind, there are no tales of derring-do involving last-minute escapes from snake pits. Snakes and snake pits are not normally involved in business adventures, except in a metaphorical sense. In business adventures there is normally money at stake, and that always brings a necessary element of caution to every business venture.

As just shown at the end of the last paragraph, the word *venture* arises naturally in a business context. It is a close cousin of *adventure*. Venture has always meant a commercial enterprise in which there is a considerable risk of loss as well as the chance of gain (*OED* definition). Commando entrepreneurs love adventure simply because there is risk. Their role in a corporation, on a specific business venture, is to take on the task that involves a higher level of risk, succeed in that task through flexibility and intelligence, and create the situation for others to enter the field with the greatest risks removed. It is exactly analogous to the role of commandos in a military operation. They create the conditions for the conventional forces to exploit and quickly scale the opportunities presented. Businesses need such people; such people have a particular temperament.

The temperament is about making rather than simply finding opportunities. It is about making adventures happen because adventures bring unforeseeable, exciting opportunities. When those opportunities arise, the commando entrepreneur is best able, by temperament and by training, to seize them.

It is worth pointing out here too that technology is often part of the adventure, simply because technology is now changing so fast and transforming the landscape in which businesses operate. Commandos are trained to a high level in the use of technology. Entrepreneurs are increasingly found in the technological sector or developing a new use for technology in their businesses. I believe it is because they – commando entrepreneurs – want to make the most value out of opportunities provided by technology. They are more drawn by temperament to design than to argument, to lateral thinking rather than to purely critical thinking. They are more inclined to see what technology could do than to be cautious about its limitations. In other words, they often have an adventurer's love of their special equipment and they enjoy exploring what can be done with the latest versions of that equipment.

There is always the need to build bridges to new opportunities. This might be through physical things or through technology, but more frequently it is through people. I do not believe that many entrepreneurs are loners, just interested in doing things their way in isolation from others. Commando entrepreneurs, in particular, are good at making bridges, forging connections, through people. They know that they have to rely on others to help them and, in return, that others are reliant on their efforts. Although strong-minded they are also good team players, and the joy of an adventure always multiplies when it is shared with colleagues who are part of the same team with the same objectives.

It is always easier to understand relatively abstract concepts through real people. What is this love of adventure and how does it show itself in people who have succeeded in the business world? In the rest of this chapter I will describe two people who understand this commando entrepreneurs love of adventure, and I give a short case study of one other.

*   *   *

An interview with Dereck Foster

I met Dereck Foster in Barbados. He is one of the island's leading business people, founder of an international company that serves the automotive sector. He is a man with a great entrepreneurial story to tell, and he tells it with a lilting voice and an occasional deep-throated laugh.

He was born to a Barbadian father who moved to Guyana with his family. However, his father became disenchanted with the political situation in Guyana and sent young Dereck back to Barbados where he was looked after by his grandparents. The grandparents were not wealthy and the teenage Dereck felt obliged to find work to help the family finances. He worked for a few companies, but the significant one was an automotive paint company. He started at the bottom, mixing paints, eventually becoming the manager of the department.

The idea for a business was forming in Dereck's still youthful brain. He took his idea – "not really a business plan, but the aim was to take the business to a different level" – to the boss of the firm. Dereck had seen where technology was moving, and his plan was to take the business in that direction. His boss was less insightful and thought the plan was wrong, too sophisticated for the users who ran vehicle body shops on the island.

In many ways it was an extraordinary statement of ambition by Dereck. The automotive paint market in the Caribbean was dominated by ICI, one of the world's biggest multinationals. Not daunted by this fact, and spurred on by his boss's rejection, Dereck started doing deals to set up his own business and bring in the new technology.

Of course, Dereck had little money, especially compared to the global resources of ICI, but he was brilliant at making partnerships that advanced his business. He had approached a local paint company that had a manufacturing plant in Barbados. From this partnership Dereck gained investment and a factory. He smiles, regretting the fact that he had to give up half the business but then laughs as he acknowledges that, 24 years later, he has the same shareholder who has lent experience and support, and allowed him to make mistakes.

There are always mistakes but you learn from them. His partner/investor placed great trust in Dereck's abilities but the trust proved well-placed. If you are good enough, you really are old enough, and business generally does not trust young talent as much as it should. This is another lesson that should be learned from the military that place their greatest trust in young people to perform on the front line.

Dereck forged partnerships with European paint suppliers. After two years Dereck's company, Automotive Art Inc, started expanding in the Caribbean and drove ICI from its dominant position. Nowadays ICI has a very small presence in the region. Automotive Art grew consistently, increasing its market share.

As with any business stories, there were twists and turns along the way, deserving a book of their own, but here we have to tell the story in outline. The short story here is that Dereck's company contracted out manufacturing and developed its own paint brand that represented 95% of the company's sales. They expanded into Latin America and set up a distribution centre in Florida. Expansion into the USA looked like the natural next step but Dereck's Dutch supplier unexpectedly sold its business.

> *"So now we couldn't sell in the States. We could have challenged it legally but at a team meeting we agreed that it would have been like taking on nuclear warheads armed only with knives."*

Remembering this brings out Dereck's deepest chuckle. Despite meeting the biggest setback of his business career, he still managed to enjoy it for the adventure it was. The outcome was that Automotive Art retreated to its Caribbean base, renegotiated contracts with suppliers and made its future more secure.

"But I had tasted what a big market means," says Dereck. "Now I wanted to see my brand on a global stage. So we looked for a global supplier and found one eventually in Poland – unlikely, I know, but it was the right company. We entered a joint venture with them, buying out one of the owners in the process. Today, as a result, we have nobody to tell us what to do or where to go. We decide."

The strategic plan had been set back by events, holding back AA's ability to grow for perhaps five years. In the Caribbean, because its market share had become so large, the company was in a defensive position. But those years were vital in holding that position, making plans and partnerships, laying the groundwork for future growth.

Dereck knew where he was heading and today Automotive Art is selling in the USA. It is a sizeable international company, with hundreds of employees, exporting to 60 countries. There is a franchised retail business. It has been quite a journey.

"The best part of the journey has been the people. There were six of us who started the company, the best people from the previous firm. Together we've created a good team through hard work, and by recruiting great people. The most important thing has been to identify our areas of weakness, and to do so with complete honesty. No one can be good at everything, we each have different skills and personality traits."

"By honestly acknowledging weaknesses we've been able to get stronger and stronger, because we recruit to fill the gaps."

"The one thing we all have in common is the will to win. We've never wanted to be in any position but No. 1 – not always possible but we have to try for it. We're all very driven, motivated to achieve that, and when we win we celebrate victories."

"It is an adventure. Every day is an adventure. I can do great things, travel the world, see other cultures. All the time, in those different places, I am struck by the similarities we have as human beings. And I still love coming to work – it's fun."

You can see why Dereck is an ideal member of the board of the Barbados Entrepreneurship Foundation. The BEF is an organisation I co-founded to encourage entrepreneurialism in this small island country. It is early days but Barbados is moving in the direction of embracing entrepreneurialism. Dereck is instrumental in that movement, with his company sponsoring an annual competition with prizes awarded to business ideas presented by the island's bright young people. Submissions are narrowed down from a short list of 20 to a final five who make a pitch. The winners receive seed capital to get their enterprises off the ground. Who knows? In time a new global company might emerge.

* * *

Frederic Cumenal is different from Dereck in every obvious way but I do believe they share a common approach to seek the new, to embrace the 'disruptive'. I was intrigued by Frederic's use of this word when I talked to him, because I did not prompt him but it seemed that he instinctively understood the special role of a commando without ever having been one himself, and applied it naturally to business situations.

Frederic is Parisian, educated at French universities and Harvard Business School. I have known him since he was running Chandon Estates in California 15 years ago. We have stayed in touch as he moved to the top jobs in Moet & Chandon and now Tiffany & Co, the legendary New York jeweller. He is a sophisticated global citizen who understands luxury global brands as well as anyone I know. He was drawn to Tiffany by the sense of hope, energy and creativity of New York itself, feeling that Tiffany needed to go out into the world and make more of itself.

He has already changed Tiffany, which now has 400 stores worldwide. He loves its New York origins but he is building a luxury global brand whose sales are already 70% from markets outside the US. Coming from Europe, he knows that luxury brands from France and Italy can have an aura that is disproportionate to their origins. Tiffany is already a global brand - that has been a given for decades - but Frederic is now driving it into new geographical markets and growth is accelerating. "We still have a long way to go, so we want to make this exciting" is typical of his thinking.

"I see there is a love of adventure. There are many things though that entrepreneurs and commandos have in common. There is a willingness to take risks without agonising over it. But there is something else in

common, it's about causing disruption behind the lines. Entrepreneurs are always trying to invent new ways, they do things differently, not satisfied with the normal way. Both commandos and entrepreneurs are not selfish but they like to operate with a small group, to keep their grip on things. Perhaps they're not so good at managing 'through the army' and all its levels and channels and processes – they enjoy touch and feel. They find a way."

Tiffany has been developing its business throughout the world. Historically Japan has been an important market, China has developed well, but the Middle East had underperformed. Frederic decided it needed a different approach.

"It seemed that we needed entrepreneurial people to relate to the entrepreneurial profile of consumers in the Middle East and Gulf markets. It's a challenge for big companies, to capture something that's outside the norms, to reach new consumers in different ways. We tapped into the profile of entrepreneurs. We had been like the army – we knew about organisation, logistics, clarity of goals, the execution of plans. But you will hit a wall if that's all you do – you need to try new things."

"You need disruptive factors, people who will create a positive kind of disruption. They are different animals, you have to nurture them. It's more difficult for them to operate with processes and planning rigor, they operate more by themselves."

"We recruited and identified people who were able to do that. In a developed market you need to deploy different strategies, so we recruited groups of people with a different profile. I suppose you might call them

> *commando entrepreneurs. They knew the area well but*
> *they were not used to big companies. But we adapted*
> *ourselves a bit to them. We did a joint venture, identified*
> *opportunities. We didn't see this as short term – most*
> *of the people are still with us. Their leader was recently*
> *promoted to be head of China, a job he does now with*
> *the benefit of three years' experience with us in the*
> *Middle East."*

It is an approach that I identify with because it expresses my own beliefs. Frederic brings his own take on the subject and would not previously have identified these people by the title of 'commando entrepreneurs'. He would deny that title to himself but optimism courses through him, the excitement of an adventurous challenge and, though thoroughly French, he is a confirmed New Yorker.

> *"I'm convinced New York is the core of the Tiffany*
> *brand. It's the one big thing that makes us different,*
> *we're ultimate New Yorkers and New York is the ultimate*
> *world city. This city is a melting pot, it has the ability*
> *to attract the most creative people, it always gives a*
> *second chance, nothing is impossible here. This is so*
> *much in our genes. The rest of the world shares that – or*
> *wishes to share that – with us. Young folks in Asia believe*
> *tomorrow will be better than today, and that's the same*
> *for New Yorkers, it was the same after 9/11, the same*
> *after Hurricane Sandy. We rise to the next challenge."*

> *"It's a fundamental belief. The world is made of*
> *opportunities. If you don't know the future you have to*
> *invent it."*

That would be a good message to send any commando entrepreneur off to a new mission.

Case study

Heineken Brazil: A taste for adventure

I first met Chris Barrow in New York in 2010, soon after he had been appointed head of Heineken in Brazil. We spoke after I had given a presentation, and Chris wanted to accelerate the implementation of his new strategy to grow Heineken's sales in Brazil. He thought we could help him gain 12 to 18 months, and we were soon running sessions with his new team. They loved the HPT sessions and Heineken sales in Brazil boomed ahead.

Chris was crucial to this. He describes himself as a lover of adventure and, since leaving his birthplace South Africa in 1996, he has lived in many parts of the world that others do not go to. He is well-suited to Heineken because this is a brand that has within it a real sense of adventure. I suggest to him that as Heineken aims to 'excite and surprise consumers' part of the brand attraction is a love of adventure shared by Heineken's own people and its beer drinkers. Heineken consumers love excitement and surprise in the brand – it becomes a natural place for commando entrepreneurs to operate and deliver that feeling.

Chris points to Heineken's history, talking of responsible beer-drinking as a social lubricant. There is a strong emotional aspect that makes this a brand loved by its loyal consumers, a sense that it is always trying to be out there in front, finding new places, connecting with new people. "In social networking since 1864," Chris smiles, linking the company's founding date as anticipating the age of Facebook and Twitter. The brand's purpose is to bring people together – to interact, to celebrate together, to sort out problems. The idea is for everyone to leave with a smile on their face, feeling better.

Chris loves adventure and he finds it in his work. In Brazil he was asked to turn around a brand that was growing too slowly. He had started the task when he ran Latin American sales operations for Heineken in 2005 for two years. At that time Heineken sold 45 hectoliters of beer in Brazil. Given the direct responsibility for Brazil in 2010, Chris raised sales to 1 million hectolitres in 2012.

"It was about high performing teams, setting clear goals, constant measuring of performance and motivation as a result. I believe in the concept of 'failing forward' – embracing mistakes, learning from them, still moving forward at momentum to achieve success."

This is a commando entrepreneur who loves adventure. He is now Chief Strategy Officer for Heineken, one of whose six corporate behaviours is 'act like an entrepreneur'.

Chapter 5

Make a difference

The third characteristic of a commando entrepreneur is a determination to make a difference. I believe this is one of the main reasons why people sign up for the Royal Marines – and why they serve and remain attached to the Marines after their time of service. Perhaps it is also demonstrated by the continuing affection shown towards the organisation, as we celebrated its 350 years anniversary in 2014.

Similarly, in the business world, entrepreneurs are motivated by more than just money. They want to make a difference to their own lifestyle but, more importantly, they wish to make their mark on the world in a positive way.

The starting point for this book was that we live in a world of change. We need to recognise that and embrace it. Although change is most frequently forced on companies from the outside, the best changes are driven from the inside. To bring about such change, you need people who truly welcome the idea of change because they want to make a difference, they are not satisfied with the status quo.

If you think change is impossible in your organisation you should probably get out. But before you do, you should question why you might lack the commitment – imagination, determination or belief in yourself? – to make the necessary difference. There is no doubt that bringing about change demands enormous energy. But not even trying can sap energy far more than making a real effort. Making that effort brings about a positive change in yourself so that, even if you fail in your objective, you succeed in growing yourself as a person.

In the spirit of John F. Kennedy do not ask what your company can do for you but what you can do for your company. If you follow that route it will almost certainly lead to greater personal growth as well as greater achievement for the company. It is a spirit that is imbued in you as a Royal Marine: you are there to serve, to embrace the values and to make a difference by helping others.

You have to set yourself goals. They stretch you, like doing a gym workout, and you have to keep stretching yourself regularly. This characteristic 'Make a difference' is a bit like a muscle, and you have to keep using it.

The objectives we set ourselves, the objectives that are closest to our hearts, are the ones that really define us as people. They are all the more powerful when they encompass what you do for others rather than just what you do for yourself. To become a chief executive is one thing; to become a chief executive to enable you to change the world in some way will take you a lot further.

Just as no 21st century business is motivated solely by the pursuit of profit to the exclusion of other objectives, so no 21st century commando entrepreneur is motivated solely by the pursuit of money. We live in a world of interdependence rather than independence. Our lives and our businesses need a strong sense of collective purpose, and that is why commando entrepreneurs are motivated to make a difference.

It reminds me of the quotation from the athlete Arturo Barrios: "If you run in the forest, plant a tree". But this philosophy is more than just 'it's good to give something back'. Commandos feel a moral obligation to help those who need help, but they think carefully how best to give that help. The greatest difference you can make is to enable people to do more with their lives after you have departed. It is the old adage about teaching a man to fish rather than giving him a fish. The best help provides the greatest support for the greatest number.

Values do matter. If you choose to do something that does social good, as well as achieving a business objective, it brings extra satisfaction. You should not be afraid to speak up for what you believe because that is what makes you different. Commando entrepreneurs are often vocal but they are more likely to clean up a beach than complain that it is dirty. They know that your actions have to show what your words mean.

Commando entrepreneurs operate best in companies that recognise this need to make a difference. This is why they work well inside a corporate environment because they wish to align their personal values with those of the company. The best companies have a real purpose, and the best companies encourage their people to make a difference individually within the framework of the corporate mission, vision and values.

Here is a man who achieves that. I know him well because he works in McKinney Rogers, embracing our values and helping our clients to understand and deliver their missions.

An interview with Nick Jermyn

Nick Jermyn is definitely a commando having trained and served as a Royal Marine. Despite his original lack of business experience, I would say he is also a commando entrepreneur. He is an interesting example and he has certainly had an interesting life; not the conventional career path, certainly not the conventional life ambitions.

Nick wants to be an actor; that is his dream. He is now 44 so he is leaving it late but if he keeps this ambition I am sure he will achieve it. Nick normally achieves what he sets out to do.

Educated at a comprehensive school in southern England, then studying History and Drama at Winchester University, Nick decided that he would join the Royal Marines. He failed to get a cadetship but went back at the end of his first year at university, winning a bursary to the Royal Marines. At university he was president of the students' union. By his own admission he was having far too good a time, including vacations working as a tennis coach in the USA.

Eventually the Royal Marines sucked him in full time. He joined as a 2nd Lieutenant and retired 18 years later as a Lieutenant Colonel. Along the way he had served in Afghanistan where he trained Afghan police in Helmand. But still he had his dream of becoming an actor.

Not many people move from the Royal Marines to the Lee Strasberg Theatre & Film Institute to train as a method actor. As well as the lure of acting, Nick was attracted by living in California. During his commando service he had experienced its natural contrasts while co-commander of the 'high readiness unit' in 2004. During this he had trained in the heat of the Mojave Desert and the snows of the Sierra Nevada. So, after leaving military service in 2010, Nick set out to Los Angeles and Hollywood to become an actor. He has taken big steps but not yet fully lived his dream.

In relation to Nick, I think of the quotation from John Scully when he was head of Apple:

> *"The new corporate contract is that we'll offer an opportunity to express yourself and grow, if you promise to leash yourself to our dream, at least for a while."*

In effect that is what is happening with Nick and McKinney Rogers. In 2013 I needed someone with the right values and entrepreneurial attitude to work with our American clients. I instinctively felt that Nick could do the job. So he has hitched his dream to ours for at least two years. After that the lure of acting might be too strong.

With Nick I hired on instinct but also on his Royal Marines background. He is a natural leader and I knew he could pass on leadership skills to senior US business people. What I was looking for was someone with values imbedded from his training and experience as a commando. Interestingly, Nick was the first to challenge me to say that such values – of a commando entrepreneur – needed to be seen more broadly. They are not, he insisted, just for the military and for business: they are values to guide lives. They help us as individuals to understand our own purpose, to realise more deeply who we are as people, to achieve our potential.

So within two months of that job interview Nick found himself, perhaps to his own surprise, running the McKinney Rogers office in Santa Monica, California. He was knowledgeable about leadership but admitted that he knew little about business. Yet here he was advising American business leaders, and of course he did it well. He is extremely good at personal relationships and at making connections.

> *"You have to go for whatever you wish to achieve,"*
> he says. *"If I'd allowed myself to be swayed by those*
> *recruitment statistics (99.9% need not apply), I would*
> *never have joined the Marines."*

> *"I decided I should not fall into the trap of telling myself*
> *'I know nothing about business'. The fact is that I have a*

wealth of experience of leadership. I realised, while sitting in meetings with corporate leaders, that what I think of as ordinary can be seen by others as extraordinary. So I always strive for excellence, and I want never to let down the people in the companies that I work with. There is mutual trust, and that comes from the values that became part of me in the Marines."

This can seem magical to others, as Nick says. He talks about leaders needing a balance of nature and nurture to perform at a high level. To a very high degree Nick embodies the true values of a commando.

"The perception of the military is often wrong. It's not about guns and killing. I joined, and I stayed, because I wanted to help people to help themselves. It's deeply ingrained in me that I will help the vulnerable and not exploit them. I want people to get more out of life. I find ways to help people not to kill them. My time in the Marines was about making a difference in that way. And if I wasn't making a difference in this current job, I would walk away from it."

"There is no point unless you make a difference."

Nick always wants that feeling, and it motivates him to be a success. A commando entrepreneur, I would say. In his business role people tell him that he has transformed their lives.

"I believe I can change someone's belief by creating greater awareness. Part of this is giving the person permission to ask for help. That is a sign of strength not weakness. You can challenge yourself to be better,

and it means you can also challenge others. Leadership is about that, it's not about the authority of rank. There is something extraordinary at times about just getting people in a room and enabling the conditions for each to recognise a common humanity. Only connect. Seeking connections is what drives me to do everything that I do."

Nick is also an example of the way you can learn, grow, develop through training. The process is iterative and continual: you have to keep learning. Literally as well as figuratively he's learned: *stand still and you're dead*. A self-critical restlessness drives him on, but it is a positive urge to improve and not become set in old ways.

* * *

Bill Simon is the recently retired CEO and President of Walmart USA. I first met Bill when I was facilitating a strategy session on Diageo's Bailey's cream liqueur some 15 years ago, and we established a natural camaraderie. There were things we had in common: Bill had been in the US Navy before going into the business world (retiring as a Lieutenant Commander), we were both believers in the critical importance of business execution and we shared a philosophy which has led towards the idea of commando entrepreneurs. Having worked with Bill through a few changes of role and company, it seemed natural to work with him again when he joined Walmart.

An interview with Bill Simon

"Many people in the business world do strategy," says Bill. "But few do execution well. It's what businesses lack. You need to be tenacious – a commando quality – to make your strategy happen, and you have to be fearless – run to the sound of gunfire, not away from it."

"What matters is aligning with the mission. It's the critical issue for business. That's what mission leadership is about and I've seen it working in companies of all sizes. I believed it would work in Walmart, although the mass scale of everything Walmart does throws up particular leadership challenges."

"We talked about this soon after I arrived at Walmart. As a result we set up the Leadership Academy, modelled on a military staff college. The aim was to accelerate the progress of talented people, to gain seven years' experience in two years. We saw young people being transformed from timid juniors to seasoned executives through this compression of seven years into two. Some of them are now vice-presidents in Walmart."

"Our thinking was that Walmart equipped managers well with technical training, but it was not so successful at training people for leadership. These are massive stores, small companies in themselves, with a thousand people working in a store. The store managers are well-paid and we could hire people from grocery stores but this was a different magnitude and complexity. We had no incubator to bring people on. That was the role of the Leadership Academy."

I ask Bill about risk-taking and adventure. How did he see these characteristics in people around him? Were there people he identified as commando entrepreneurs?

"The love of adventure is closely tied to risk. We're adrenaline junkies. A risk-averse personality leads to a lack of adventure, a lack of confidence means you seek safety. That's not going to succeed in business. I'm constantly pushing people further – very rarely do you have to pull anyone back."

"It is linked too to making a difference. You must want to achieve more than picking up the pay check. When I joined Walmart, I looked at the healthcare business – this was 2006. The high cost of prescription drugs was a problem in the US and around the world. Canada and the UK subsidised the cost of pharmacy medicines but in the US the drug companies and pharmacies charged high prices. In my first three months I decided Walmart would lower the cost of generic medicines to $4 per unit."

"I had no idea if it would work but I was sure it would be worth achieving. I remember going home and saying to my wife 'this might be the shortest appointment of my career'. She said to me: 'What better way to get sacked?' so we did it, and it worked brilliantly. We knew within 15 minutes that it would work, it caught on like wildfire. Although we had planned its introduction to last over a year, we had to roll it out in weeks."

"This made a difference in a number of ways. It reset the market for generic drugs – Walmart had that market-changing power. This brought reputational advantages to Walmart and it saved money for our customers. Ordinary

American people have saved $7 billion in medication costs since we took this approach."

"The thing is, on a price of $4 you can still make 20%. Most of the costs had been institutional costs, but they could be eliminated – they were the unnecessary costs of filing a claim. Some pharmacy companies didn't like it but we managed to partner with many others – and the market has now changed without question. That has made a difference, a big difference to the lives of most people."

"You have to seek personal fulfilment. I worked at Pepsi and it was the most fun I had in any job. But I wasn't fulfilled, I was selling sugary water to people, not getting enough satisfaction for myself. I've done other jobs – public service for Governor Jeb Bush in Florida – which were fulfilling but not materially rewarding. You try to find a balance, and Walmart was one of the places where you could find both."

"Recently we launched a programme for US manufacturing, aiming to bring back manufacturing that we had lost to Asia. The mathematics were moving in our favour, meaning that it became feasible to bring production closer to the point of consumption. Wages and demand were going up in Asia, but wages and household income in the US were flat. Transportation costs globally were soaring but we now had cheaper energy in the US – as well as the obvious access to an enormous home market."

"This means that there are manufacturing categories where it is now efficient to produce products in the

US that had been made overseas for years. We took a position with our suppliers, recognising that they needed a longer term commitment and investment. Walmart had normally bought a season's worth of goods. Now we made a longer commitment, for example building a plant in Georgia rather than sourcing goods from Asia. The US had not manufactured towels domestically since the 1980s – now we found we could make them and sell them for the same price as in China. And our sales were 40% higher with 'Made in USA' labels. The workers in those factories were Walmart customers."

"Make a difference. It works. It helps you achieve more if you aim high. Average just gives you average – I wish we could ban the word. Everything you do, do it with all your might."

* * *

To round off the chapter on making a difference, here is a short case study about Damian Perl whose interview is in Chapter 3. Here I focus on one aspect of Damian's story that demonstrates what makes him different.

Case study

Global Strategies Group: making your presence count

Damian Perl and I share some similarities apart from our first name. We were both trained as commando officers. I was briefly one of Damian's instructors when he was going through training but then our paths diverged for 20 years. In the intervening time Damian Perl had founded and grown Global Strategies Group to become a multi-million global business working on the design and supply of resources (increasingly software) for commercial and national security systems.

That is a fascinating story covered in Chapter 3. Here I am focusing on one aspect of that story because it shows several facets of a commando entrepreneur, in this case the desire to make a difference. Damian Perl left the Royal Marines to join the Special Forces – "In your mid-20s life's an adventure". After that, what should he do? He found himself working on security programmes, most notably in Africa. These required, as shaped by Damian "a cerebral approach, not muscle on the gates".

He returned to London at the end of the 1990s and set up his own business. At first he operated from his back room, then from a small office, but everything was going slowly. It was hard to break into the entrenched establishment of recognised suppliers. But things changed after 9/11 in 2001.

After the shock of 9/11 Damian saw an opportunity to use his skills and experience to do some good. People wanted to get to Afghanistan but they had no means to do so. Damian was being approached to help, and he had contacts in the region with companies, individuals and humanitarian organisations like the Red Cross. An Australian news company contacted him, one of many enquiries from people wanting to get into Afghanistan. "What do we need? How do we get there?" Damian knew that if he could create the way to do this, other things would flow.

He took himself off to central Asia with not much more than a mobile phone, travelling overland by hitchhiking into Kabul where he took a room in a bombed-out hotel. He had a single-minded focus and discipline, as well as a lateral way of looking at things. He was there to solve a problem. He did that by leasing a plane and setting up the first non-military airlink between Afghanistan and the outside world at the time. He recognised the need and met the requirement with innovation and speed. It turned into a business and, using smaller planes, he started flying in people from humanitarian organisations and governments wanting to set up embassies.

Of course, he had to make the routes secure and he established links with the UN. When eventually it was time to hold elections in Afghanistan, Damian's company was given a leading role in their organisation and security.

By the end of this period, Damian's Global company had become a business with hundreds of millions in revenue. But the satisfaction for Damian was not derived from the finance:

> *"We were saving and changing lives. That was the important thing. When you are helping the UN run elections, allowing millions of people to vote for the first time, that gives a huge sense of reward."*

Damian Perl proved that he could make a difference, a vital motivation for commando entrepreneurs.

The Commando Entrepreneur

Chapter 6

Achieve the extraordinary

So you are not frightened by taking risks and you enjoy an adventure. You also want to make a difference. These characteristics set you firmly on the road to achieving the extraordinary, which is the fourth characteristic of the commando entrepreneur – and the theme of this chapter.

We all want to achieve. No one sets out to be an under-achiever, no one really wants to be simply ordinary. We all value our own individuality and few of us believe that we are really just like everybody else: there is something in our individual personality and DNA that sets us apart. Yet few people manage to achieve the absolutely extraordinary. Some individuals can (and we value them highly), and those individuals also have the effect of inspiring and helping others, as part of a team, to achieve extraordinary things.

To achieve the extraordinary you need to start and finish with energy. The qualities of the tortoise and the hare have to be combined. Speed and stamina are both needed. It is better to finish one task brilliantly than to leave a hundred tasks not quite done.

If you believe you will achieve. Believe in your own potential and raise your sights far above the ground in front of you. It is always possible to be ordinary, almost without trying. It takes effort and imagination to be extraordinary.

You might dream in your sleep but you only realise dreams by your own efforts when you are awake. It is vital to keep that sense of a personal dream alive in your thinking so that it leads to action. In the business world the dream becomes a vision and the mission becomes the way of realising that vision. Even though the vision has personal meaning, a relevance found in it by each individual, there is an element of the universal that enables all the members of a company to relate to it.

So military and business campaigns need visions that inspire individuals and inspire teams to deliver their own missions within the framework of the whole. Everyone plays a part, but the leadership skill is in identifying who are the people best equipped to play particular roles.

I argue for the commando entrepreneurs to play breakthrough roles in a business. These commandos might be the equivalent of special forces but they are reliant on other people around them in a business. It should never be them and us, with individuals or groups placed on a pedestal.

A leader's expectation should be that everyone in your business can achieve whatever they set their minds to. If you have no expectations of your people, they will achieve very little. Expect the extraordinary and you will find people stepping forward to deliver.

What happens when a commando entrepreneur delivers? You celebrate the achievement, acknowledging all those who have contributed. Pride is always better when accompanied by humility. There is always a joy in achievement; it is a more powerful motivator than money itself. But then, as commando entrepreneurs, you move on to the next mission. Clausewitz, whose thinking provided the basis for modern military strategy, urges us to look on each engagement as part of a series. There are always new missions to achieve, new worlds to explore.

Human beings are creative. We have imaginations that allow us to see possibilities that might never have been thought of before. Commando entrepreneurs especially are by nature creative. This does not mean that they are gifted artists or musicians – although they might be – but that they enjoy the challenge of a problem that needs to be resolved. Finding that solution, and carrying it through to a conclusion, is what I mean by extraordinary business execution. The extraordinary is seldom achieved by a repetition or imitation of something that was done previously, so you use your imagination to think beyond the obvious, to break away from a formula.

This gives you responsibility, and by accepting responsibility people earn respect. If they are trusted to do a certain task, that brings responsibility with it, which they rise to. A leader should never give responsibility and withhold trust. Only by giving responsibility and trust will you discover what that man or woman can achieve – and the more you give, the greater the chances of achieving the extraordinary.

Commando entrepreneurs are always willing to accept responsibility. If they fail, it is their fault, but they aim to learn from mistakes. If they succeed they are humble and this earns respect far more readily than bragging.

These are lessons learned from training and serving as a commando. When you are on a difficult mission, probably in unfamiliar terrain behind enemy lines, you have to trust those you are with. It is a matter of life and death. The consequences might not be fatal in a business situation but the need for trust is every bit as vital. It means that you have to know – by experience, by evaluation, by training – that the people you select for a task can be trusted. You need to know that they are true commando entrepreneurs.

As part of that giving of trust, you encourage the exercise of initiative to achieve the mission. The commando entrepreneur thrives on initiative because it allows him to follow his own instincts, to use his creativity.

How do you know that what you have achieved is extraordinary rather than simply very good? It is a judgement that you and others will make. Often it is hard to define in advance because the truly extraordinary is probably a picture that has not yet been actualised. At the same time you have to have a picture in your head of what success will look like.

In business, targets are set most of the time by numbers that can be measured – market share, competitive position, volume of sales, increase in profits and so on. In the first place, make these measures stretching but not impossible. Then, in the second place, if you exceed those targets by significant amounts, you will have achieved the extraordinary.

To achieve the ordinary you have to do things right; to manage well. But to achieve the extraordinary you also have to do the right things; to lead well. The commando entrepreneur understands the need for both, but will always aspire to the extraordinary.

Let me illustrate these thoughts with the case of Jin Iwamoto, who has interesting experience working in Asia, where the idea of the commando entrepreneur might not be expected to be immediately accepted.

An interview with Jin Iwamoto

Jin Iwamoto was a rising star of the Japanese business world, gaining leadership positions in major global companies in his thirties. First he was regional vice-president of Wilkinson

Sword Schick, then MD of Diageo Moet Hennessey. In Japanese terms this was extremely young, particularly in a culture that has tended to revere the legends who, by the age of 70, have won the right to a hearing for their business achievements.

But at the age of 44, Jin was restless and questioning whether he should continue trying to climb the ladder in multinational corporations based in Japan. He was aware that 'we have only one life' so he decided to do something extraordinary. In thinking about 'what next?' his thoughts turned to the US and China.

At this point I met Jin and was impressed by him as a person. I had not yet (this was 2008) formed the idea of the commando entrepreneur in my own head, but in retrospect Jin completely fitted the mould. I offered him the challenge of running McKinney Rogers in Asia.

> *"No one knew McKinney Rogers," says Jin. "Who are they? Explaining didn't help because it raised even more doubts in the minds of Japanese people. It came from another culture and there seemed little connection with Japanese thinking. It also came from a military background and people were wary of that. My father was particularly sceptical – he couldn't understand why I should give up what he saw as an exceptional career for such a risky situation."*

I am glad Jin made his decision to join us. It was not easy but Jin wanted to do something different and to make a difference. He felt that he had previously done the expected, that there was nothing unique in his successful rise to the top of the corporate world for global companies. Here, though, was an adventure, the chance to do something extraordinary. No one had done this before in Japan.

It helped that Jin was an absolute believer in mission leadership, following **The Commando Way** philosophy. He felt that mission leadership was especially appropriate for the Japanese business situation. It starts with the need for an inspiring vision, which leads to clarity of mission that flows through an organisation. Jin had started to apply this in Japanese companies and he knew that it worked. The more he worked with it, the more he believed in it, because examples were proving its effectiveness.

There was his own personal vision underpinning this too. Jin's ambitions are not confined to his own success in the business world. He is ambitious for his country too. He has had a lifelong ambition to make Japan strong, an ambition perhaps sharpened by the economic history of Japan during his working lifetime. In the late 1980s Japan was a global star of the business world, admired and envied by other nations. But then the economy turned down and it seemed that successive political and business generations could do nothing to put things right.

> *"It was not just the economy. There was the feeling that the secret of Japan no longer existed, there was no mystery, and there was certainly no strong leadership. I wanted to change that for the next generation."*

Jin was disappointed in Japanese business leadership. He told me stories of going to global conferences where the Japanese leaders did not speak up, did not take leadership positions, did not even express opinions. This was not because they were not able to think, they just did not know how to demonstrate leadership. They were unwilling to speak loudly so they simply sat quietly and smiled. This upset him and made him determined to achieve his vision to make Japanese business and its leaders more visible and more willing to play a key role in the global business world.

He saw mission leadership as potentially the universal method that would move towards that position. But there was a big gap between his position and those asking 'why should we listen to foreigners and military guys?' It is a fair question. They were saying that surely there must be something closer to Japanese culture.

Jin took the positive out of this. It meant that there was no competition in Japan to the idea of mission leadership. So he forged ahead and has been converting Japanese business leaders to the way of working. He believes that the more clients who use mission leadership, the more Japanese business leaders there will be to achieve his vision. Once they have mastered the principles, they are immune from the criticism that this is not sufficiently Japanese. It becomes Japanese through the successful examples that are increasing all the time.

> "Actually I think we probably use the military background more than in any other part of the world where McKinney Rogers operates. It works because people relate to its discipline, they like the clarity of purpose and the teamwork it engenders. It is still exactly as it would be explained in any other country but has become natural here."

Jin is not military himself. He was not trained in any of the services, but he is trained in the martial arts. I think that was a strong point of connection for him. He came from a strong

Karate background, practised to a high level for ten years, and coached his university team. It meant he became used to working in extreme environments, and he accepted the discipline and dedication needed. Although he was not being trained for military combat he was trained to be determined in his personal and business life.

When I ask him about the extraordinary vision of making a difference not just to himself and to businesses but also to his country, he finds it less extraordinary but completely natural and logical.

> *"If we focus only on securing more clients and winning more business, we won't achieve enough. There has to be more. We have to spread quicker to a mass understanding. I am now 50 so I have 20 years to make this difference and do something extraordinary. Time is always limited so you have to push yourself."*

Jin is now interested in Internet workshops that will spread his business message faster and to more people. He cites the example of a professor giving a talk on the Internet with 20,000 people listening in. The technology interests him as a different way of doing things, and perhaps this will increasingly become the way, with less need for face-to-face meetings. We will see but Jin will find out through making it happen. He believes it is time to expand our thinking because in two years we will be behind this generation. As in the military, if you do not have the latest weapons, you are likely to lose.

Jin is a good example of a commando entrepreneur. He also works with many too and he told me a story of one particular Japanese business (which needs to remain anonymous). The company covers many sectors but the focus is on food. Having succeeded in the Japanese market, a man was appointed by the company to run the business in China. The business had not been doing well; many Japanese companies struggle to make money in China. The man appointed spoke no Chinese and he did not speak English to a high level, but he had mastered mission leadership.

Jin was not sure that this would work. For example, the use of the *Gladiator* film seemed to stretch the possibilities of cultural differences too far. Speaking in Japanese, using military examples, showing ancient Roman armies in a Hollywood production. Surely the Chinese would not be able to relate to this? But it succeeded because a vision was created that people could identify with; and this enabled missions to be made that people understood and strove for. The language barrier was overcome by good translation.

The Japanese leader in this Chinese company succeeded because he was trusted by his senior team in Japan to deliver high performance through mission leadership. The Chinese company turned around, as the Japanese company had previously, by staying true to the principles. Jin found it impressive because it proved to him that mission leadership was a fundamental, global and universal methodology for business. Even so, he was still surprised that the Japanese leader stuck so rigidly to the principles, never doubting or deviating in any way. He had adopted it as his own.

I asked Jin why – apart from the financial evidence that it worked – was this adopted so wholeheartedly by his Japanese client?

"It's about freedom and constraints. I think that is what really made its mark on him. He needed to give freedom to his people and to delegate several layers down. At the same time he needed to establish and communicate

a clear mission from which there could be no deviation. Otherwise it would be totally uncontrolled. He had experienced this working in Japan, and he thought it would work just as well in China. It did because it established and showed the need for trust, to give space to people in the company, while also setting boundaries."

This takes us very close to the definition of a commando entrepreneur. There is something in that seeming contradiction in these two sets of words – commando entrepreneur, freedom plus constraints – that expresses the spirit I am seeking in businesses.

* * *

I now want to give an example of a commando entrepreneur who is completely unlike Jin. Jin is Japanese, male and (on the surface at least) unemotional. Maggie Timoney on the other hand is Irish, female and ebullient. Yet both share the same characteristics I explore in this book, and both of them have my absolute trust to tackle difficult jobs.

An interview with Maggie Timoney

Maggie is the MD of Heineken Ireland, having also played various senior roles with Heineken in North America and Europe. Maggie is a very interesting woman who has consistently achieved great things in her business and personal life.

Originally born in County Mayo, Ireland, she went to the USA in the 1980s on a basketball scholarship at Iona College. They now remember her with some awe as a leading scorer elected to the hall of fame and 'one of the greatest women's basketball players in the history of the program'. She gained an MBA in the USA so her student time there was productive.

After working in one or two other companies, she took her skills and experience to Heineken USA. Heineken then put her in a number of commercial roles in the Netherlands, Canada and USA before making her head of HR in the USA. It was while she was in that job – Chief People Officer – that I met her first.

> *"Heineken in the US was doing a lot of work on strategy and culture," Maggie explains. "We had spent a lot of time on the cultural issues, the softer side such as Myers Briggs. But everything, particularly the culture, needed a shake-up. There was little trust in the management, there had been at least three CEOs in four years, the climate was bad and people were afraid. Dolf van den Brink, who was the new MD, and I talked about what we needed. I remember Dolf saying 'Damian McKinney, he's so tough, he goes for the jugular to make things better'. That was something positive for us – after all, our first value became 'Be brave'."*

Heineken decided to take its people off-site in Connecticut and they asked me to run some high performing team (HPT) sessions. Maggie was unusual for someone in the HR role – there are not that many who say 'let's go to the bar'. She was very confident in who she was. We got on well together and Heineken started to rebuild the trust it had lost. It was mainly a case of doing some simple things that Maggie led. She made Dolf much more visible to all employees – for the first time there was a meeting for the whole company. She gave equal hours for culture and strategy, and involved people in thinking about the issues of the next ten years, as she describes:

"We had to bring people on the journey, and we had to make some swift decisions about the people who were not on the bus. Some would say one thing in a meeting then something different when they went out the door."

"We all decided on the principles we would adopt. The first was 'Be brave'. Then 'Decide and do', 'Front of the pack' and 'Take it personally'. We arranged a global conference at Harvard and people really bought into these principles. They helped us break down the silos. There was a moment that was like the light going on."

"The HPT work involved field exercises that were important. You helped us realise that the way we behaved in the field had to be the way we also behaved in the boardroom. These were the best team exercises because they got everyone in the team discussing then putting it together as one code."

"The difference the HPT process makes is that it lives on, much more than anything else I've been involved in. it means you go naked in front of each other (not literally!), seeing each other's strengths and weaknesses in an open, honest way. You see different people leading at different points, and that's OK. It doesn't diminish the role of the leader. The leader has to be comfortable with that and it becomes a brilliant way to harness a team's energy and intellect."

"So we were brave, we took risks. And we were resilient.

That's a vital quality. Externally there will always be stuff thrown at you, you get knocked down but you get back up. You're fighters, you've got a backbone."

Of course Heineken recognised and regarded Maggie's role highly. She was appointed as MD of Heineken Ireland – her own country but a challenging job. Most people will think of Ireland as Guinness's own kingdom.

"I was quite clear from the start that I wanted to stretch people and push boundaries. I wasn't here to take it easy. 'Fail forward' was our phrase. Don't worry about failure, as long as you learn from it and try not to repeat the same mistake."

"It's interesting that people seem to have this image that an MD must be serious, pondering things intently and in isolation. I decided I just had to be me – I am who I am. I laugh, I joke, I shout. Mine is not the traditional way. I need to inject fun, excitement and adventure into my work. Work should not be safe and dull."

"Early on I said to some of my marketing team that we should plan a trip to New York. I wanted them to break out of the box, open up to a different culture, be less focused on the small, traditional ways. If you stretch yourselves you have fun. And I know those HPT teams meant people had a lot of fun but also did things as a result."

"Even if Damian made me jump out of a plane – which terrified me, but I did it. Fortunately a parachute was provided."

"So in Ireland we now get people thinking big. We brought the whole company together at the O2 in Dublin,

Dave Stewart of the Eurythmics played and everyone danced. I was interested in his book on creativity The Business Playground. Simply, everyone had a great time, but it really helped our themes of accelerate, creativity, innovation."

"People ask me about being a woman in a male-dominated business world. To be honest, when I sit in a room full of men, I don't even think 'I'm the only woman here'. I never think that. I certainly don't think I should act in a certain way, swinging a big thing like some men might. It probably goes back to growing up in County Mayo and, if you wanted a game of basketball, you had to play, the girls and the boys together. We made a team."

"The feedback I get from other women is 'My God, I'm so glad you're not trying to be a man'. Of course I don't, that would fail. Just act as you are. I'm not following a script from the leadership books. Authenticity is important, I just try to be myself and people like that."

Maggie is a natural leader. She is great fun to work with but she demands a lot. She will never accept the 'OK', she always wants to do more. I will simply say watch that space in Ireland where she is taking on a big company, Diageo, with a world-renowned, locally loved drink, Guinness.

"I don't spend my days worrying about what they're doing," Maggi says. "Of course we think 'what will Diageo do' but we are clear in our vision and mission over the next five years. We are going to be the most exciting and innovative drinks company in Ireland. We're really going for it."

"We're going to launch more brands, moving away from being a mono-brand. We can't just rely on Heineken lager, we need more in our arsenal. But we've stood still too long. The external conditions changed but we didn't. It will be tough, there will be some pain, but we will achieve what we set out to do."

What Maggie sets out to achieve is extraordinary. It will make waves. Business associations, consumers, employees will notice and will come to recognise Heineken Ireland as an exciting, innovative company. Maggie is the proof that commando entrepreneurs are not defined by their gender.

* * *

Finally, one more short case study about a company and a man who aims to achieve the extraordinary.

Case study

Grohe: aiming for extraordinary growth

I began working with David Haines when he was CEO of Grohe, a company that originated in Germany in the 19th century. The company, like many, had its ups and downs over the decades, with several changes of ownership, but had survived by developing a range of sanitary ware and bathroom products. The days of family ownership had now gone, and David had been brought in from a private equity environment with the task of growing the previously stagnating business.

David's instincts are entrepreneurial. He has never been a commando but he thinks like one. He wanted to grow the business and make it a force in its market in Europe and worldwide. He makes demands on himself; he also makes demands on his company and colleagues that seem unreasonably ambitious to some. But he has an absolute clarity of vision and he delivers to that. Joining Grohe in 2004 he was determined to make the company the fastest growing in its industry by 2012. He succeeded.

In 2014 a Japanese holding company, Lixil, acquired Grohe for over 3 billion Euros. David became chairman of Grohe within the Lixil Group, looking to build on the growth strategy that had transformed the business in less than ten years. Grohe had acquired a Chinese company, Joyou, and with other Lixil companies centred on Japan, the US and Australia a global strategy was needed.

I attended a meeting in Hong Kong that brought together the key executives of Lixil Group companies in bathroom product areas. These people were from four companies that had previously been competitors. Now they were required to work together on a joint strategy. In the meeting David quickly seized the initiative and proposed an unreasonable vision. But, of course, it was perfectly reasonable to David.

I participated in and observed the meeting with some fascination. David's own colleagues, perhaps more used to his trailblazing approach, thought the idea was exciting and began exploring it. New colleagues from Japan, the US and Australia reacted in different ways: silent bemusement, a preference for more incremental improvement, a guarded welcome but uncertainty overall, no doubt a little fear. Over two days David shaped the new strategy that was then taken to a meeting in Shanghai with the Japanese Group CEO. One of the Americans observed after that meeting that he had never before seen a CEO tear up his own vision because he recognised that the alternative was so much better.

David is a commando entrepreneur who always wants to achieve the extraordinary – even if the extraordinary can appear quite ordinary in his eyes.

Chapter 7

Are you a commando entrepreneur?

In the previous chapters I have explored the characteristics that make a commando entrepreneur. I have given some examples through interviews and case studies. So I hope that you will have a good feel for what makes a commando entrepreneur. But what about you? Are you one? Do you want to be one?

I thought it would be helpful and interesting to set out a scenario for you to respond to and test yourself. It is probably not to be taken too seriously but it should help you think through some of the questions that might be in your mind at this point. All you have to do is read the scenario (inevitably it's general not specific) then decide which are the three most important actions you would take in response. Each of the answers is given a points rating which I will explain after you have answered the questions in response to the scenario.

The scenario

You are in a global company that intends to launch a new consumer product. Let's call it Product X although it will have a distinctive brand name. The plan is to launch it first in one pilot market then to distribute it worldwide. But it could fall at the first hurdle if the pilot launch is a flop.

You have been selected by your boss to bring Product X to market and make it a success. Success is defined by a sales target that seems extremely ambitious but the resources allocated do not seem to reflect the potential that the company anticipates for the product. The pilot is in a market you don't know, and you sense a resistance early on to the new product from the in-country team – everyone is very busy and morale is not high.

What do you do?

Choose three of the following

- Go back to your boss and ask him to knock a few heads together

- Work on a detailed case for the allocation of more resources, then lobby the people who can release them

- Start making a plan, fully thinking through all aspects of the mission you have been given

- Decide that time is short and you need to start getting people on board by persuading them of the product's potential – and asking for their advice

- Thank people for all helpful advice you get and ask them to continue as sources of advice

- Come up with an innovative launch idea and broadcast this to see if people volunteer to help out

- Build a network of colleagues who could influence the product's reception, keep expanding the network, and keep refining your plan

- Locate yourself in the territory where the product will launch and shadow sales reps on their visits to build your own understanding of the market

- Time is very short and you're not sure you will be able to meet the deadlines for the pilot so you decide to go straight to a full launch to maximise impact

- Start looking for another project because this one has such a high risk of failure – and you're not even sure it deserves to succeed.

Now rate your responses

1 Get your boss to help

How will your boss react to this? He has trusted you to sort out a problem and now you are asking him to invest his own leadership capital on your behalf. Perhaps he will be willing, if the product really has that potential. But it will be better to hold him in reserve by first trying to make better progress on your own behalf. You need to win a few hearts and minds by yourself, then think about how you use powerful supporters further down the line.

*Commando entrepreneur rating: **0 points***

2 Make a case for more resources

It's always good to be very clear about the resources you have and what, ideally, you might need. But you might spend a lot of time on an unproductive effort if you go down this route. The outcome might be that you delay yourself and that means delaying the product launch – but you have already been given an unmissable timescale. This option might seem prudent but it is not really why you were chosen for the task. You should think positively and creatively about how to get the most out of limited resources.

*Commando entrepreneur rating: **minus 3 points***

3   Start making a plan

Absolute clarity of mission is your first requirement. You need to establish exactly what it is if it is at all unclear, then you need to think it through to formulate a plan in some detail. If you start thinking about this it will soon be good to test the outline of the plan with close colleagues. They will almost certainly improve it and give you confidence that the plan will work. But always remember, even the best plan might soon need to be adapted so do not get dogmatic about the details.

*Commando entrepreneur rating: **4 points***

4   Ask for advice

As part of your planning you will have worked out the key people you need to have firmly on your side. You might also need them to contribute people and resources so it will be better to involve them early on in a positive way – rather than to demand further down the track. New thoughts will emerge that might help you modify your plan – be welcoming to these suggestions and incorporate them if you think they improve the plan. Set yourself a time limit – you should by now be working to a time schedule – because you need to deliver on time.

*Commando entrepreneur rating: **3 points***

5 Thank people

It is always good to express gratitude. People are more likely to help you again and it might just help dissolve any hostility you encounter. Take all advice as well-meant – even the most negative-sounding might have a point. Keep people on your side as much as you can. Most people – particularly if they are in the same company – have a natural inclination to support the common good. But in the end, it is your decision, your plan, and you will not be able to please everyone.

*Commando entrepreneur rating: **1 point***

6 Innovate and broadcast

No doubt it is good that you are thinking creatively but you need to think through all the implications. Some people might salute your idea, but many might not. There is too great a danger of setting off internal resistance, as well as the possibility that an idea shared widely and prematurely will leak outside. You could scupper your own plan by alerting your competitors. Come up with ideas, by all means, but share them with your close group – and ask for specific volunteers.

*Commando entrepreneur rating: **minus 2 points***

7 Build a network

You will need allies. You probably have more than you realise so you should keep lists and contact details. It is always good to keep people informed lightly and regularly – even a sentence or two at the coffee machine. Your network – ever expanding – is your best asset and you must use it fully.

Commando entrepreneur rating: *3 points*

8 Locate and learn

You need to know the ground where you will be operating, but in this case you have little knowledge of the country. It is sensible to use local sources to provide information. In any case there are people you need to be working actively for your cause. A little humility in looking to them for information and guidance will pay dividends, and you will soon to get to know the market better. That knowledge will help you develop your plan further.

Commando entrepreneur rating: 3 points

9 Go straight to full launch

What this means is that you have really messed up your timing. An essential part of planning and execution is to allow enough time for proper preparation. You should never aim to launch without an operational rehearsal – you will have created a big risk that should have been avoided.

Commando entrepreneur rating: minus 4 points

10 Look for another project

Or, probably, look for another job. It sounds as if you really did not invest any personal effort or commitment to make this project succeed. You were given an opportunity, and you failed.

*Commando entrepreneur rating: **minus 9 points***

How did you get on?

Add up the points scored from your three choices.

A minus total: *you might make it as a first-class bureaucrat*

1-3 points: *you have some way to go*

4-7 points: *look for a mentor and you might make it to become a commando entrepreneur*

8-10 points: *you are a commando entrepreneur but you will need to keep working at it.*

Chapter 8

How to make a commando entrepreneur

To answer the question in the chapter title, we need to start with commando training. How do the Royal Marines go about the training of a commando, and how do the qualities instilled through training fit with or add to the qualities of an entrepreneur?

The first thing to be said is that there is a commitment to training in the Royal Marines that would be seen as exceptional in the business world. To pass out as a Royal Marine, to earn the right to wear the green beret, requires extraordinary commitment. Each recruit is personally tested, physically and mentally, and the tests are difficult and exhausting.

Behind that is the belief that each Royal Marine needs to be trained in a way that will ensure that the cohesion and performance of the whole Corps is maintained at the highest level. It is, after all, a matter of life and death when a commando is sent into action straight from training. You simply cannot afford a weak link in the chain.

Most outside observers of Royal Marines training make two main comments. First, how tough it is; you really have to be special to survive it. Second, how much support each trainee is given to come through the training. There is no doubt that everyone is subjected to the toughest physical and mental challenges at high intensity over many months. You need to be very strong and resilient to graduate. But having graduated you will be equipped to deal with the toughest challenges that might be thrown at you, whatever you go on to do in life, inside or outside the military.

It is true that each recruit is given the best possible support to succeed. Royal Marines training is not a case of sink or swim. There is no thought of quickly sorting the men from the boys to hone the group swiftly to a hard core of natural commandos.

The recruits are given every chance to become a commando. Everyone is helped by the Royal Marines who are training them and also by their fellow recruits. Because everyone is in this together – genuinely – and there is an incredibly powerful team support system that helps to pull people through. There is a celebration of the recruit who seemed destined to fail but finally made the standard – and, during the period of training, many of the recruits have a period when they seem bound to fail. If they eventually get past that point to succeed it is usually down to mind-set rather than physical endurance.

The trend in business over many decades now has been to recognise the ever-increasing need for conceptual skills. Businesses need people who can think and imagine and then act, because this is the way you solve problems and seize opportunities. There is a need for speed too because unsolved problems and lost opportunities can quickly kill off a business. Businesses need to invest in people and that means they have to invest in the training of people – women and men.

Businesses can, and do, approach this as a purely cerebral activity but one learning from Royal Marines training is that physical activity sharpens your mental skills. Sam Moreton, later in this chapter, has some interesting thoughts gained from his own experience of taking part in the 1664 Challenge. Business people have to think and they have to act, and training needs to cover both aspects. A strategy is useless if it is not executed well. That, for me, is the overriding business imperative addressed by *The Commando Way.*

Businesses need winners. But, of course, winners are not made in gyms or on assault courses. Those activities refine what already needs to be there inside the individual: the drive, the commitment, the vision. In the end, this is what makes a fully trained commando – the discovery of something special inside yourself. Training is directed to that aim, rather than simply measuring the number of seconds taken to climb a rope. Training is really measuring an individual's desire. No winner is ever casual about winning.

Winning is fun. People enjoy achievement. Commandos are motivated by the will to win, and so are commando entrepreneurs. The pleasure gained from achievement is experienced by the individual but it is always magnified when the achievement is shared with a group.

The strength of the group

Let us look at one example. 2014 was the 350th anniversary of the founding of the Royal Marines. To commemorate that landmark, and to raise money for a charitable cause, the 1664 Challenge was devised. Volunteers were invited from the serving ranks of the Royal Marines. The Challenge was for a core team of six, one from each unit of the Marines, to carry out every element of the task. Then further volunteers were recruited to join in and perform one of the different physical challenges. The overall task was daunting.

1 *Ski*

The team would ski 1664 km in full survival kit, from the north of Norway inside the Arctic Circle to Stavanger in southern Norway. This would require the equivalent of a daily marathon on skis, and would take place at the end of winter, from February to early April.

2 Sail

At Stavanger the team would immediately set off to sail a yacht 1664 nautical miles to Cadiz in southern Spain. The time involved would be 27 days to enable the third phase to start on 30 April.

3 Cycle

The team would then cycle 1664 km through Spain and up through France, across mountains and plains and all terrains to arrive in Cherbourg in northern France after 21 days.

4 Canoe

Without rest, the team would then jump into kayaks to canoe across the English Channel to Portsmouth, a total of 100 miles in busy sea lanes, to be completed in 30 hours.

5 Run

Again without pause the team would run around southern England and much of Scotland to places associated with the Royal Marines. This would require the team to run 1664 km in 58 days, completing 18 miles per day between the end of May and the end of July.

The whole 1664 Challenge would culminate in a moonlight marathon around the streets of London, with a final march and welcome into the city.

Quite a challenge. One of the marines who volunteered and was selected to represent his unit of 600 was Captain Sam Moreton. Sam had joined the Royal Marines three years previously, having graduated with a degree in Philosophy, Politics and Economics from St Peter's College, Oxford

University, followed by a year working as an electrician – an interesting mix of intellectual and practical skills. Now, three years later, he is accompany second in command at 42 Commando Royal Marines based in Plymouth. He volunteered for the 1664 Challenge having seen a notice pinned up on the board.

> *"They were looking for a combination of physical robustness and mental attitude," says Sam. "I'm a good athlete and rarely get injured. I actually enjoy mountain training, being up to my knees in deep snow while carrying heavy kit. But there was no physical test to qualify – I guess they knew the physical records of people applying. Perhaps the mental attitude – assess from interviews and references – was more important. This was about how you socialise, what you're like in a team, your ability to interact with others."*

The objective was to encapsulate the commando spirit and Corps values in a significant physical and mental challenge. In doing so, the aim was to raise money for the Royal Marines Charitable Trust Fund to help marines injured in action and to ease their transition into civilian life. £350,000 was raised. As Lieutenant Colonel Gary Green, one of the driving forces behind the 1664 Challenge, put it: "we wanted to show the Royal Marines Way. As hard as you can, as fast as you can. As much a mental as a physical challenge."

The Corps team comprised six marines, including Sam Moreton. This team would be the central one, chosen to carry out all the different phases of the Challenge. They had a month's training to prepare them before setting out in wintertime from deep inside the Arctic Circle. I was interested in Sam's thoughts about the Challenge – what his reflections were, what he gained from it, what were the differences between the activities, what might be lessons for those outside the Royal Marines?

"Obviously you need determination but determination is a form of stubbornness. It's the refusal to believe that you bit off more than you could chew. The drive to get you up every day. You get that from the Marines. Training wheedles out those who lack it. Determination is not taught. The Corps allows determination to flourish, you're taught ways to succeed."

"There was never any support in the 'don't give up' sense on the Challenge. No one had those sort of doubts, everyone was there to complete the Challenge. You shared the experience, the shared burden makes it OK. It's like when you're yomping you draw strength from others struggling, look around, think I'm all right. You never want to be that bloke who's struggling at the back. Here we had a group with no one struggling at the back."

"Marines are individualistic, strong, driven, they don't want to ask for help but they're always willing to help. You have to break down the 'don't want to be a burden' mentality. If you take off the pack from the man at the back you take something away from him that destroys him and destroys the team."

"What I found hardest on the Challenge was other people. That's always what it's about. For the Corps group it was relatively easy, we shared our commando background. But there were other contributing and

sometimes that was difficult. Being told what to do by someone you dislike is a challenge – generally that was someone outside the Corps. In the Corps there's a homogenous feeling, even though there are all sorts of differences in backgrounds, likes, dislikes, politics, taste, education."

"What you're doing dictates how you interact with others. You ski in single file, the leading skier works 30% harder than the rest because he's crushing the snow that then becomes easier for the rest to ski. You have to shout, you're in your own little world, you need to do it at a low enough intensity to get up and do it again next day. The solitary nature and low intensity leaves space in your head. I thought about everything, it was a reflective time, time out."

"Sailing is a completely different situation. You have four on watch, one at the wheel, you're crammed tight together facing each other. It's more conducive to talking or you can sit in silence. It changes the dynamic of the team, makes for more social periods."

"With the cycling, you're working harder, the available space in your head goes down. You're close to others and you chat. You can talk to the bloke next to you, then change positions, it's part of the team effort in cycling. But there's less spare mental capacity because you have to keep concentration to avoid obstacles in road, to cope with changes of direction, the climbs up or down."

"With the long runs we found it easier to run in a big blob. If you run in files you can't escape the bloke next to

you, the effort becomes harder."

"It's all about team dynamics, learning what works in different situations. You determine how people react socially and how they interact. It makes you think about the arrangement of people in other situations, perhaps nothing to do with physical activity, the seating arrangements for a dinner, who to pick for certain tasks in a team."

"I don't think the Challenge changed me as a person but it changed what I know. I learnt a lot about myself and about other people. It was the same six men, from start to finish, all sharing a common aim to achieve the distance."

"Others were responsible for planning, logistics, and it was important how we interacted with them. You learn how people work as individuals, how to get the best out of others. As a bonus I have now met and spoken to every senior person in the Corps."

"You're in the challenge together, you share hardship and you get very close to the people in your team. After a few months you talk to each other in ways you wouldn't at first. You started talking about personal things, like your dad, and that's OK. But you get incensed when anyone outside the group talks in the same way. You have allowed that familiarity to those in the same situation but others can't come in and assume those rights."

"In the business world you might have a failing business, in special measures. You have to respect that the team

dynamic already exists – you can't be over-pally or you run the risk of looking like David Brent. A new boss needs to be aware of existing dynamics, not throw weight around. Your power comes from the person not the rank. You have to earn respect."

"The Corps team of six was given the hard physical part. They didn't have to organise, they simply executed the task. The organisers would make a plan, present the proposal and the good ones would ask 'how do you want to change it?' Sometimes it was too ambitious, sometimes not ambitious enough. The best people involved us in how to execute the plan."

"Strategists and planners are rarely the people who execute the plan. If they don't listen to those who will execute it, it's pointless. The man doing the job is in the best position to say how best to do it. Give people scope to say what will work."

"All this is straight from the Corps, at the heart of Royal Marine training and I guess you can take it directly into a business situation. You have your mission. The best plan never survives the first encounter. People are the biggest difficulty."

"We had well-intentioned people who believed it was their job to help us do what they thought was impossible, so they tweaked and suggested variations to 'help us'. There are natural differences in conditions, terrain, slopes, etc. so they started suggesting variants like 'just do 14 miles on this stretch because it's really difficult'. Our response to that was: 'What do you mean? We run

18 miles'. No shielding, no cushioning was asked for. Running 18 miles was our mission and we knew we had to stick to that without deviation."

"As a leader you have to understand this - you can't change the goal. We weren't saying 18 miles a day was unachievable – we did it, we knew we could. Never compromise the mission. Look at what you need to achieve and stick to it."

* * *

What you see in Sam is a commando and, I believe, a commando entrepreneur in the making. He exemplifies some of the apparent contradiction in the term. I would describe it as an individualistic team player.

I think of others that I know who are a little further along the career path, with a few more years' experience, now making their way in the business world.

Robin Simpson, for example, grew up in Zimbabwe then came to the UK at the age of 20. He joined the Royal Marines two years later, training as an officer then serving in UK special forces (the equivalent of US SEALs), particularly in the Middle East and Afghanistan.

When he was leaving the Marines some years later, he went through the transition process that is now established. Jokingly he likens it to preparing prisoners to join the outside world. "What's out there? What have I got to offer?" these are common but worrying questions for people leaving the service. The same questions worry generals as much as ordinary soldiers.

Robin became a business consultant, based in Canada. He soon discovered certain truths:

"You step into the unknown, do as much planning as you can, take one step at a time. But you realise that you do know what you're talking about. What works for one client might not work for another, so you appreciate the need to be flexible and innovative. I'd say conventional forces follow set procedures, special forces don't. So my training and action in the Special Boat Service has helped give me those mental skills."

"One of the main challenges in business is facing up to the competition. Every business is aware of its competitors; every business needs to be. But businesses need to think of the boundaries that exist and challenge how real they are. You might not be able to shift the obstacle but you can shift perception of the obstacle. The most common obstacle that people perceive in business is the competition – the companies and people out there who are trying to beat you. So you can help people rethink that obstacle, giving them the confidence to overcome it by seeing the old problem in a new way."

"This helps you, as a person in the business world, to make a difference to people's lives. There's a lot you can do through training. In the military 95% is training, 5% is real execution. The proportions are reversed in business. So it's really rewarding when, after a day working with business people, someone comes up to you afterwards and says: "I tried so hard to get out of this, I couldn't see

the point, but I'm now so glad I did it, it was one of the best experiences of my life."

Robin has learnt a lot, and is applying it every day in new situations. He also exemplifies another point – you never stop learning. There is a constant imperative to train and to retrain. Otherwise the world moves on and the world moves past you.

* * *

Further into his business career is Trevor Parker, who left the Royal Marines in 1991. He and I served together in the same troop of 40 Commando in Belize. We have stayed in touch because, as Trevor says, service in the Royal Marines creates a strong bond.

When he left he started doing consultancy work advising local government on disaster recovery. He was spotted by a Yorkshire-based entrepreneur, Paul Dixon, who offered him a job in his car dealership business. Despite being recruited purely on a hunch, Trevor helped grow Dixon Motors plc to a £100 million company that was acquired by RBS in 2002.

After that he became known as a troubleshooter, the guy who did business turnarounds; he helped stabilise and reconstruct struggling businesses. This suited Trevor's commando training instincts, focusing him on "How do I achieve the best result?" He went into a lot of hostile business environments where the staff initially did not want him to be there. But he got them back on board, focused them, motivated them to rebuild the businesses. His mantra became "It's not about me it's about us". Trevor is a man who can walk into chaos and create order. He is a team builder, a motivator who supports people and gets things done.

"All of this comes from the Royal Marines," Trevor believes. "It's specifically a Royal Marines thing. Other parts of the military don't have such flexibility. I've seen other military men who lack the skills to recognise the needs of a situation and adapt their style to it. The Royal Marines do that, they are exceptionally entrepreneurial. It comes from the Code of Conduct which is completely transferable to the business world. It means you are able to assess situations and take command. Others agree to follow, and that makes you a leader."

"When I first went into business I thought I would have to operate in a completely different way. Initially I tried to relearn everything, I devoured business books and courses, trying to reprogramme myself to be a manager. But then I was dropped into a difficult situation, told that there was a problem and was asked to fix it. What else could I do but fall back on commando training? And it worked."

"The training continues to help. It helps me be decisive, particularly if quick decisions are needed though I prefer to follow a process, take time and make plans. I can then coordinate the team to execute the plan, giving them the confidence to deliver. In the Marines everything is training, there's a constant process of briefing and debriefing. In business – in too many businesses – things seem to happen by accident, the thinking process is not joined up. People go on leadership or management training but often they are just admin courses."

Trevor identifies valuable characteristics and ways of thinking that he has carried over from the Marines into business life. He is quick to point out the ability to respond to situations. It is an ability to be aware of the situation and to spot opportunities – then act as a result. To think and ask yourself the question: How can we best achieve this task with the constraints we have? The Royal Marine is always thinking through what are the effects we are trying to achieve? It helps if you apply that even to simple situations in the business world: What do I want to get out of this meeting? He is expert at adapting his manner to get the result he wants.

Trevor has an interesting final point to make:

> *"Royal Marines get bored easily. In that way they are entrepreneurs too – the flair is always there and the wish to have an entertaining life. You have to have fun in business. Most entrepreneurs simply want to enjoy what they do."*

Trevor is currently one of the management buy-out team at Motorway Direct. He is in line to be chief executive, after the MBO, of one of the UK's largest motoring companies. He is creating the strategy, selling the story, raising funds from investors. And making a difference for those around him.

* * *

To round off this chapter I wanted to get a view that was much more from the outside, from someone I did not know and who has had no connection with me, with commando training or with the concept of a commando entrepreneur. John Ainley is someone I had not met but I knew that he had been Group HR Director at Aviva (a multinational financial services and insurance company). For the last couple of years he has been a leadership coach. I wanted to find out if the ideas in this book made sense to him and if the characteristics of a commando entrepreneur could be seen in business leaders that he had worked with.

John's first point was that a large number of business people had an instinctive reaction against the commando or apparently military aspects of the proposition. Many people set their minds against the possibility of learning from the military.

> *"There is a prejudice – I might well have it myself," he says. "But the aspect that seems most easily acceptable in the business world is the need for a clear mission. In my work, I try to help people become clearer about their purpose. Why are you here? Why are you doing this job? It helps if you are doing it for a reason that you believe in. that can be at a grand philosophical level or just at the level of being clear about your role in a particular project. It is a fundamental need across the business world, and increasingly recognised over the last 20 years."*

> *"Risk is difficult. Since the financial crisis, businesses have become much more risk-averse. Particularly in the financial services industry they have had to, it's been a demand put upon them for understandable reasons. Big companies are trying to mitigate risk because that is a regulatory requirement. For the larger companies in particular it means that things have become more*

anodyne. But you don't create anything unless you invest in risk."

"I guess this is where the spirit of adventure could seem attractive as a counter to that. Many managers and leaders would shy away from it, but the braver ones might embrace it. In my work as a leadership coach I have become more and more aware of the loneliness of the leader in a corporation. These people really are on their own for so much of the time, and you realise the humanity, including the human frailty, of any leader. You only have to talk to them one to one to appreciate that."

John thinks that a sense of adventure would benefit many leaders, particularly in helping them develop the quality of resilience that he sees as so vital to the modern business leader.

"You get knocked back, you get knocked down, but you have to get back up quickly."

The CEO is so wrapped up in the business, there are so many people to please – shareholders, regulators, customers, employees. The individual leader is the focal point for their attention, which drives leaders to be more internally focussed. Often there are doubts – what is the right decision? Because your focus has shifted to the other end of the spectrum from your first job, where you knew who you had to please – your boss. Now how do you make sure you can still allow enough space for your own needs and satisfaction? It helps if you love what you do, if you find it an adventure. But often that desire to be adventurous is suppressed.

The Commando Entrepreneur

Perhaps, I wonder in response, the individual needs to release the sense of adventure in himself or herself, perhaps it is a matter of empowering others to be more adventurous, to be more entrepreneurial, to undertake the adventurous breakthrough tasks that suit commando entrepreneurs.

John is interested too in the need to 'make a difference'.

> *"It's more talked about, even if a little cynically. But there's no doubt that the world is looking for this in its business representatives. The drive to do good is a counter to the criticism of excessive rewards and it can be a powerful attraction to government, regulators, shareholders and customers if businesses – and significant people in businesses – strive to make a positive impact on the world, to have a point of view. It can be the sign of a true leader."*

A big feature of John's work is to do with the psychology of individuals and teams. Each individual has, as he puts it, different wiring. He talks of an introverted client who sees a problem in everything as opposed to another client who sees no barriers, only possibilities. The latter is much closer to the commando entrepreneur.

John is a reflective man, and he encourages reflection in those people he coaches. The conversation makes me reflect again on the thoughts of Claudio Fernadez-Araoz in the *Harvard Business Review* that I mentioned in Chapter 1. His thesis is that, as we live in such a volatile business world, the 'right skills' of a business person might not remain the right skills throughout a career. So, after generations of judging and selecting people on the basis of their physical attributes, their qualifications, then intelligence and their competences, we are really now in a new age, the age of potential. Businesses need to select people who have the potential to adapt to whatever changes happen in their working lives. Flexibility is all.

I would say that this is a quality taught by commando training, which brings us closer to a conclusion in the final chapter.

Conclusions

I started out with a hypothesis that I wished to test by exposing it to a number of people in the business world. My hypothesis was that there are individuals in the corporate environment who are able to perform more difficult, breakthrough tasks because they possess characteristics that are shared by commandos and entrepreneurs. I put forward four characteristics, explored in separate chapters 3 to 6, through interviews and case studies.

For the most part, for these interviews and case studies, I chose people and companies I know well. I felt these people embodied the characteristics; working with them had inspired the hypothesis. I also knew that they would be perceptive commentators, able to shine the light of their own thoughts and experience on these questions. I chose the people because I thought of them as commando entrepreneurs, as models for this role. By interviewing them, describing them and setting out what makes them special in their way of thinking and acting, I hope to have made clearer what a commando entrepreneur really is. It is a title that encompasses diversity. There is no set mould into which every commando entrepreneur fits. Indeed, if they did they would no longer fit the description because commando entrepreneurs need a mental agility that constantly tries to break free from standard formulas and expectations.

Validating the characteristics

From these interviews I believe that the four characteristics have been validated through the words of these commando entrepreneurs. Although I have placed them into individual chapters that focus on one particular characteristic that they seem to represent most strongly, it will be clear to readers that each individual exhibits all four characteristics. None of them is daunted by risk, indeed they welcome it as part of life. This attitude feeds into the sense of adventure that they share in their approach to life and work. The old phrase "anything for a quiet life" would not apply to this group of people. They relish life, and they love work that provides a rush of adrenaline. That prospect gets them up in the morning.

But they seek more than the conventional rewards of money and status to drive them on. They need a deeper purpose in their life, including their working life. I expressed this as the desire to make a difference. They have a bigger picture of the world and they wish to contribute to that picture. This creates a powerful combination of personal and corporate purposes. The connection of the two takes them onto a different plane of performance, driving them to attempt more. By attempting more, they often succeed in achieving the extraordinary. None of these people would ever be satisfied with settling for the ordinary.

Mental agility

In exploring these characteristics a number of points have arisen that provide fresh light on what makes a commando entrepreneur. Most important of these is the recurrent highlighting of mental agility. This is certainly a quality that I endorse as essential for commandos. I described in *The Commando Way* the prime need for commandos to be creative in their thinking. This has been recognised by military strategists throughout human history. During my own Royal

Marines training I was introduced to the writings of the ancient Chinese commander Sun Tzu. His book *The Art of War* remains a wise, practical and philosophical approach to military practice. For example, opening the book again, almost at random, I found these words:

> *"The direct approach is used for attack, but the oblique achieves victory."*

That is as clear a statement of the commando philosophy as you can get in one sentence. Commandos are trained to think their way around a problem. The full-frontal assault, all guns blazing, is rarely the most effective. If that is true of the commandos, it is a trait shared by those with entrepreneurial instincts. Entrepreneurs bring energy, resilience and cunning to the achievement of business objectives – and they also bring an absolute determination to succeed. By combining these shared characteristics, you produce commando entrepreneurs who succeed, above all, by their mental agility.

It strikes me too that in those earliest and most archetypal of stories, told by the ancient Greek poet we call Homer, there is a true commando entrepreneur. Odysseus is different from the other warriors around him – different from, for example, the more obviously heroic but self-absorbed fighter Achilles. Odysseus, often given the epithet 'wily', was a leader **and** a team player. He constantly used his native cunning to find his way out of difficult situations – for example, escaping from the cave of the one-eyed giant Polyphemus by using sheep as a disguise for himself and his men. He succeeded by taking on the most difficult of missions and thinking his way through them. As he did so, he showed the most remarkable resilience, another quality that becomes even more powerful when combined with mental agility.

My approach is not that of an academic but I am always interested in the changing trends of academic theory. Professors in schools of business and management investigate leadership, and publish articles and books that set out how companies can be more effective. They provide advice based on evidence and analysis of leaders and companies that they study. I have been struck recently that there is an increasing focus on concepts such as learning agility – defined as "ability and willingness to learn from experience and subsequently apply those lessons to perform successfully in new or first-time situations". This, says a white paper by Dai, De Meuse and Tang in the *Journal of Managerial Issues*, is what we look for now in leaders.

Another paper by Claudio Fernandez Araoz was published in 2014 in the *Harvard Business Review*. Under the title '21st century talent spotting' the author writes that 'uncomfortable assignments will accelerate growth for talented individuals'. It is no longer desirable to lay on a straight ladder to the top; you have to test people's resilience and mental agility by placing them in situations where their true mettle will show. For me, this is the same as using commando entrepreneurs to carry out breakthrough tasks.

The article goes on like this towards its own conclusion:

> *"Geopolitics, business, industries, and jobs are changing so rapidly that we can't predict the competencies needed to succeed even a few years out. It is therefore imperative to identify and develop people with the highest potential. Look for those who have a strong motivation to excel in the pursuit of challenging goals, along with the humility to put the group ahead of individual needs; an insatiable curiosity that propels*

them to explore new ideas and avenues; keen insight that allows them to see connections where others don't; a strong engagement with their work and the people around them; and the determination to overcome setbacks and obstacles. That doesn't mean forgetting about factors like intelligence, experience, performance, and specific competencies, particularly the ones related to leadership. But hiring for potential and effectively retaining and developing those who have it—at every level of the organization—should now be your top priority."

This is similar to my own thinking and relates also to the theories of Scott Snook, a US Army trained professor of business administration at Harvard. Scott suggests that AQ or 'adversity quotient' might be more important than IQ or EQ in getting results in business. People who manage adversity well – as a problem to be solved – have an inherently positive disposition that serves them well in the business environment. They can react to the kind of adversity created by constant uncertainty and change by being positive and agile in their mental attitude – again, I would say, the behaviour of commando entrepreneurs.

This leads to the interesting question of positivity, another subject of increasing attention in the seminar rooms of business schools. For example, this is from the website of Ashridge College, one of the world's leading schools of management.

"Positivity gives a new outlook on life. It is as essential to the well-being of humans as light is to plants....people who are experiencing any of the positive emotions think

more broadly and find more things they would like to do. They are better able to see the big picture in any situation, without losing sight of the details."

A positive outlook comes naturally but it can also be instilled by the right leadership. During my own military career I was sent on many different missions, taking many different roles that often took me out of my own zone of familiarity. I embraced the challenge of each one, loved what I did, and learnt something from each that helped me achieve more on subsequent tasks. You have to be positive. It is part of the commando entrepreneur DNA, helping you in your relationships and creating a sense of 'we' rather than just 'me'. This becomes part of the mental agility that is needed to succeed in corporate environments.

When looking to recruit, from these investigations of characteristics, I would add three qualities you should seek in candidates: mental agility, resilience and positivity.

Within the corporate environment

As I established from the start, I see commando entrepreneurs as people who operate in the corporate environment. They are not lone mavericks who resist all aspects of corporate culture, agitating to break free from corporate bondage to pursue their own personal enterprise. These are people who can bring value to corporate organisations because they know that teams can achieve more than individuals.

The corporate environment is, however, changing. It is less hidebound and less inclined to follow a command and control style of management. It is learning to welcome innovation and initiative rather than exclude them for not following procedures. There is a necessary give and take that enables more creative approaches. The prize of improved performance is brought closer as a result.

Businesses can, however, do more to make the corporate environment more accepting of people like commando entrepreneurs who will venture more and achieve more. If businesses wish to aim for better execution, going beyond the ordinary to the extraordinary, they need to spot, recruit and nurture commando entrepreneurs, enabling them to flourish. The rewards for the business are potentially great. My remaining conclusions look at areas where the corporate organisation has to provide encouragement and establish the framework for talented people to thrive.

Freedom within boundaries

Commandos – and commando entrepreneurs – by nature and training enjoy the freedom to think for themselves. But, though it sounds counter-intuitive, they also appreciate being given limitations and boundaries. The commando entrepreneur is not going to be the one demanding limitless resources. He or she will welcome the idea of strict boundaries – which might mean a tight budget.

It is about finding the best way to release creativity. Few creative people actually wish for a completely blank sheet of paper, a brief with no details. There is increasing evidence that points to the liberating creative influence of constraints. I was intrigued, for example, to read a newspaper interview

(Guardian, 30 August 2014) with the Chief Executive of Lego, Jorgen Vig Knudstorp. Lego is a company that has reinvented itself by refocusing back onto the core product – play bricks for children – that brought it originally into existence. Things had gone wrong in the early 2000s when too much diversification and invention took the business off track. Knudstorp insisted that his R&D and design teams should use fewer bricks in more permutations – a constraint that was originally resisted but that has been vindicated by business results. He commented:

> *"Many creative people are finding that creativity doesn't grow in abundance, it grows from scarcity – the more Lego bricks you have doesn't mean you're going to be more creative, you can be very creative with very few Lego bricks."*

Organisations need to find the right balance of autonomy. Unbridled autonomy could lead to actions that are inconsistent with the strategy of the firm. These lead to uncertainty and failure. On the other hand, central control is more autocratic in nature, proscriptive in operation. "Do it this way" takes away from the entrepreneurial spirit and empowerment of people. So the idea of "freedom within a boundary" is key to the balance.

The boundary can be, for example, that a business prioritises certain brands in certain markets, maintains a level of pricing that supports the margins, ensures that any local creative work is consistent with this strategy, and provides context for what the business needs to accomplish. Then they allow the operational autonomy on <u>how</u> to get it done. So, commercial teams may be able to set their own goals, localised distribution strategy, and introduce local creative work that is targeted at specific audiences and profiles. And much more, their creativity spurred by the clarity of the framework.

Speed of decision-making

This needs to be encouraged within corporations, making it part of the accepted corporate mindset. It probably requires little explanation or justification but most businesses could improve their efficiency by improving their decision-making. Companies need to look at the processes by which they make decisions – they might be shocked by their complexity.

Of course, a quick decision is not necessarily a right decision. There will always be situations where it will be right to take time, assess options, weigh up the pros and cons through a more considered investigation. It is perfectly acceptable to make the decision to wait. That is a decision without dithering, and it is dithering you need to avoid. You can think of it as a tactical pause.

An analogy might be made with the Formula One race where driver and teams have to make decisions according to the unfolding race. At what point do you pull into the pits for a tyre change? Do you come off in the next lap, take a tactical pause (even though it might only be seconds) or do you press on at full speed with the possibility, increasing lap by lap, that the tyres will explode and put your car out of the race?

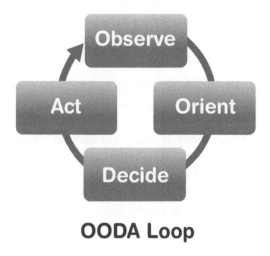

OODA Loop

Situational awareness

Context is all. The decisions you take (as above) depend on all the different factors that surround you. So businesses need to encourage their people to truly understand situational awareness. This is not a complex idea and can be explained simply (as it was to me in my commando training) by the OODA loop.

Think of the classic situation of a ladder leaning against the wall of a building. As you approach it, what do you do? First you observe it, you notice the ladder is there, you gauge its size and angle, and you realise that you have to react to it by going around, under or over it. Second, you orientate – you see that there is a paint pot on top of the ladder, you take in the height and angle and the ladder's closeness to the road. Then you decide – are you going to go around or under it, weighing up the risks. Finally you act – you go under it and the paint does not fall on you because you do not touch the ladder. Then you go on, and the loop goes on with each situation you encounter.

Commando entrepreneurs look for points of leverage. They try to understand the root cause of a problem, they think deeply to gain insight. That insight drives their response.

From a business's point of view, you analyse situations and plan how to deal with them. Particularly interesting is to get inside the thinking of your competitors. You are in the same market so there is much of their situation that you understand. Put yourself inside their OODA loop – you can anticipate their plans and disrupt them. Keep one step ahead, it will disconcert them. This can be particularly effective when your competitor is launching a new product.

Situational awareness becomes an ingrained habit that serves you in many different ways. You should never underestimate, for example, the importance of social skills. Commando entrepreneurs develop these because they know such skills help their cause. By weighing up a particular situation, it helps you to understand and empathise with the feelings of people who are part of that situation.

Clarity about purpose

The most important boundary of all is that of the company's purpose. If the company is not clear about this it can expect its people to exercise freedom in ways that are in contradiction to what your company really would like to achieve. But how will you know if you have not clearly stated that purpose? It is absolutely fundamental, and all the principles of mission leadership that commandos follow will flow from clarity of purpose.

What are you trying to achieve? This is the question that you should use in every situation – from the highest strategic level to the conduct of an everyday meeting. If you do not know what you are trying to achieve in a meeting you really should question why you are holding it. If you really do not know what your business is trying to achieve, your problems are even deeper.

You need to do something about it.

* * *

Final word

The corporate world is subject to many constraints. There are uncertainties, risks and problems wherever you look. What then should people in corporations do about that? It seems clear to me that they should seek out, then develop and nurture, talented individuals who can deal best with uncertainties, who are not thrown off balance by risk and who enjoy the challenge of solving problems. These are people to cherish, allowing them to flourish in a corporate environment.

I call them commando entrepreneurs, and they come in all shapes and sizes, in either sex, at any age. They are a diverse collection. Some of them may stand out, others have to be sought out. I have tried in this book to help you spot them, find them, encourage them, harness them. They are a special breed but there can also be something of the commando entrepreneur in every individual in your organisation – if you encourage that spirit in your business. If you do, it is my belief that your business will grow, prosper and set itself on the path to achieving the extraordinary. That is what I am interested in for every business I encounter. I have no interest, and no business of any worth has any interest, in settling for the ordinary.

Let me conclude on a personal note. I have never had a bad job in my life. I have been very lucky, you might say, but I would counter that I have never chosen a job in my life; I have tried to make each of those jobs a fulfilling job. I have simply responded to the choices others have made for me, but I have responded with a determination to make the most of the opportunities that were presented to me in this way. I love adventures, I love the surprise of not knowing what might happen today. Often I feel like a little boy, excited by the possibilities that lie ahead but absolutely enjoying the moment.

How do you unlock potential? The greatest challenge is to unlock potential inside yourself, discovering skills and abilities you didn't know you had. You discover them by being thrust into uncomfortable situations not of your own choosing. When you find this potential inside yourself it becomes easier to unlock it inside others. By doing that you create self-belief and confidence, and you instill it in those around you. That makes a difference.

Biographies

John Ainley

John Ainley is the managing partner of the Alexander Partnership, Europe's leading provider of executive coaching, leadership and culture development. He has built long term, deep trust partnerships with the world's top executive coaches and thought leaders; honing his signature – a genuinely authentic approach to helping leaders simultaneously grow and lead exceptional people with purpose and profit.

He is a coach and advisor to CEOs and Executive Committee members of some of the UK's largest companies. He equips these leaders for the enormous demands of a senior executive career. He is plain speaking, saying what he believes to be true, but always with care for the receiver.

John regularly works with FTSE 100 executive teams to help them be more effective as a team and deliver business results with greater speed and effectiveness.

One of his most significant distinctions is his ability to help a leadership team craft a strategy that engages leaders and their followers to deliver change and real business results with agility, pace, resilience and consistency.

Chris Barrow

Chris Barrow is the Chief Strategy Officer, HEINEKEN International, Amsterdam, The Netherlands. Chris was appointed Chief Strategy Officer of HEINEKEN International, and a member of The Executive Committee, in August 2013. He joined HEINEKEN in 2004 and has held a number of roles including: President Grupa Zywiec, HEINEKEN's majority owned Polish business; President HEINEKEN Brasil; MD

HEINEKEN Latin America. Chris, born in Zimbabwe, but grew up in South Africa, is a Chartered Accountant, having graduated with a B Comm. (Hons) from the University of Cape Town.

He served articles with Coopers and Lybrand (now Price Waterhouse Coopers) and worked for Distillers Corporation and The South African Breweries in a variety of roles in South Africa, Asia and Central America prior to HEINEKEN.

Frederic Cumenal

Frederic Cumenal is Chief Executive Officer of Tiffany & Co. Prior to joining Tiffany in 2011, he held senior leadership positions at LVMH Group, most recently as President and Chief Executive officer of Moët & Chandon.

Before joining LVMH in 1995, he served in various general management and marketing capacities for Procter & Gamble, the Ferruzzi Group and Mars.

Frederic is a graduate of Institut d'Etudes Politiques, of Ecole Superieure des Sciences Economiques et Commerciales (Essec) and of Harvard Business School.

Martin Davis

Martin is currently the Chief Executive Officer of Kames Capital plc. This follows a number of high profile roles at key financial institutions and businesses, including CEO of Cofunds Ltd; CEO of Openwork Limited; CEO of Global Life Emerging Markets for the Zurich Group; CEO of Zurich International

Life; Commercial Director of Sesame Limited; Executive Vice President of Corillian Corporation's Internet Banking software business outside the United States; and Director, Strategic Planning at Reuters.

Martin served for 9 years in the British Army, attaining the rank of Captain. Commissioned from the Royal Military Academy, Sandhurst in 1982, he spent the latter 5 years of service within the Special Forces Group working closely with various HM Government agencies and Intelligence Services, and with operational roles in Northern Ireland and the Middle East. Positively Vetted to Top Secret level.

Martin secured an MBA from London City Business School and Diplomas from the Institute of Marketing and the Market Research Society, graduated in 1991. Martin has a keen interest in sport, having competed at national level as a schoolboy in athletics and subsequently representing the Armed Forces at various levels in hockey and rugby. He still plays competitive hockey in the Hampshire Open leagues.

In 1996 Martin led a 2500 km cycle across Europe, from London Bridge to Marrakech, to raise £100,000 for a cancer charity. Still involved in many charitable and sporting events. Member of the Crondall and Ewshot PCC and Finance sub Committee.

Dereck Foster

Dereck Foster, is the co-Founder of Automotive Art, the Caribbean's largest automotive after-market retailer. He served as its CEO between 1990 and 2008, and is currently the Executive Chairman of the Automotive Art Group. Automotive

Art has four (4) company owned stores in Barbados, two [2] in St. Lucia and Franchisee operated stores in seven [7] other Caribbean countries.

In 2002, Automotive Art opened sales & distribution arm in the USA, that supplies over thirty five markets in the Caribbean and Latin America.

In 2006, the company acquired Marshall Trading – a 25 year old lumber and building supplies company in Barbados.

In 2012, Automotive Art concluded a joint venture acquisition of an automotive paint manufacturer in Poland that produces Automotive Art's private label paints – this acquisition has catapulted the Automotive Art brand onto the world stage, and has enabled the Group to market products in sixty-five countries across the globe.

Dereck was born and educated in Guyana and has won several awards including the Ernst & Young Entrepreneur of the Year Award for Retail & Distribution. He has served as President of the Barbados Manufacturers' Association and currently serves on the boards of several companies outside of the Automotive Art Group, including Goddard's Enterprises Ltd, the West India Rum Distillery, The Crane Hotel, and the Barbados Entrepreneurship Foundation.

Dereck's passion for Entrepreneurship led Automotive Art to start its annual Entrepreneur competition which helps entrepreneurs bring their ideas to life.

David Haines

David Haines, the CEO of LWT, successfully managed the sale of GROHE to LIXIL Corporation in 2013.

David was appointed CEO of GROHE Sarl in 2004. Under his leadership, the company has become Europe's largest and the world's leading provider of sanitary fittings with a prelim. turnover of € 1.58 billion in 2014. David spearheaded the successful restructuring and transformation of GROHE in the years 2005-2008, implementing a business model that focuses on profitable growth and innovation, cash-flow, state-of-the-art production and cost management.

Since 2011, also Joyou AG, the market leader in China, has been owned by the GROHE group allowing the company to benefit from a second global brand. David serves as a member of the Supervisory Boards of Joyou Grohe Holding AG and Joyou AG.

Since 2012, David Haines has been a Non-Executive Director of Imperial Tobacco, a FTSE top 20 company, where he serves as Chairman of the Remuneration Committee and is member of Nominations and Audit Committees. He was previously Chairman of the Board of Directors of Vimpelcom A/O, the NYSE listed leading Russian mobile phone operator.

David served Vodafone Group plc as Global Marketing Director before he joined Grohe, and holds first class honours degrees from the University of Greenwich, London.

H. Jin Iwamoto

As CEO of MHD Diageo Moet Hennessy, Japan's top luxury wines and spirits company, JIn transformed a company with 14 consecutive years of decline into one with three consecutive years of growth. Prior to that, he was VP Asia Pacific of Schick Wilkinson Sword, where he led the company through M&As under Warner-Lambert, Pfizer and Energizer to maintain its position as #1 in the market. Also, as the company's first Global Business Director, he created its first global brand identity, package and new product.

Joining McKinney Rogers in October 2008, Jin brings his experience of managing complex organizations, M&As and joint ventures and is a professional of organizational transformation. A proactive community member, Jin was coach of the Karate Team of Tokyo Institute of Technology (1988-1996) and chairman of PTA at Setagaya Yahata elementary school (2007-2009). Jin graduated from Information Science Department of Tokyo Institute of Technology.

Nick Jermyn

Nick joined The Royal Marines (RM) in 1992 as a Bursar with a BA (Hons) in History & Drama from Winchester University after spending a sabbatical year as Student Union President. During eighteen years of service he travelled the world, commanded Yankee Company, 45 Commando RM and The RM Landing Craft Branch whilst deploying operationally in Sierra Leone, Kuwait & Iraq and Afghanistan where he operated as the Chief of Staff , Security Sector Reform within Task Force Helmand. He is Arctic trained, a Jungle Warfare Instructor and Amphibious expert.

He has represented the Royal Marines at Rugby and Tennis and retired in 2010 as a Lieutenant Colonel before moving to California to pursue a lifelong ambition to act. After training at The Lee Strasberg Institute in West Hollywood and working with Mckinney Rogers as a Leadership Consultant he secured his green card and now lives in Santa Monica, California working as an Actor and Leadership Mentor and youth rugby coach.

Nick is a Francophile with an apartment in Perpignan and enjoys paddle boarding, reading fantasy novels and good red wine.

Bill Simon

Bill was President and CEO of Walmart U.S. from 2010 to 2014. When he joined the company in 2006, he led the team that created and launched Walmart's $4 prescription drug program. In 2007, Bill was named COO for Walmart U.S and held that position until he was appointed President and CEO. As CEO, Bill was responsible for over $280 Billion in revenue and1.2 million associates. Additionally, he has been a major driver in the resurgence of US manufacturing. He developed and led Walmart's initiative to buy $250 billion in US manufactured products. A passionate supporter of veterans, Bill was instrumental in the company's pledge to hire any returning veteran.

Prior to joining Walmart, Bill held several senior positions; Brinker International, Diageo, Cadbury-Schweppes, PepsiCo and RJR-Nabisco. He also served in the public sector as Secretary of the Florida Department of Management Services appointed by Governor Jeb Bush. Bill was responsible for the state's operations and administrative functions, including health care benefits, human resources, the Florida retirement system, facilities management and real estate.

Bill currently serves on the boards of Darden Restaurants Inc, the Foundation for Excellence in Education and the Barbara Bush Foundation for Family Literacy.

He served 25 years in the U.S. Navy and Naval Reserves and attended the University of Connecticut, where he earned a Bachelor of Arts in economics and an MBA in management.

Maggie Timoney

Maggie Timoney is currently the Managing Director of HEINEKEN Ireland, starting in May 2013. A seventeen year veteran of HEINEKEN she began her career at HEINEKEN USA in 1998 as National Sales Planning Manager. She also served as Senior Manager - Strategic Planning & Distribution leading to the restructure of the entire HEINEKEN USA distributor network.

In 2001, she transferred to the Netherlands where she held the global position of Senior Manager, Distributor Management for HEINEKEN International. In 2006 she was appointed General Manager of HEINEKEN Canada, Inc where she drove the substantial growth of the Heineken brand, resulting in Canada becoming one of the brand's top ten markets in the world. In 2010 Maggie returned to HEINEKEN USA as Chief People Officer where she worked closely with her CEO on the business and culture agenda leading to the turnaround of HEINEKEN USA's business.

Prior to joining the Heineken Group she worked for E & J Gallo Winery and an Anheuser Busch wholesaler both located in New York.

Maggie is a graduate of Iona College, New York, receiving both Bachelor of Arts and Master of Business Administration degrees. While at Iona, she starred for the women's basketball team. In March 2013 she was inducted into the Naismith National Basketball Hall of Fame, an honour reserved for the basketball greats in the USA. Maggie also captained the Irish Women's National Basketball Team.

A native of Ballina, County Mayo, Ireland, she is married with two children.

Dolf Van den Brink

Dolf Van den Brink is President and CEO, Heineken USA, Inc., White Plains, NY. Dolf was appointed President and Chief Executive Officer of Heineken USA, the nation's premier beer importer, in October 2009. He joined the company following a successful four-year tenure as the Commercial Director of Bralima, Heineken's operating company in the Democratic Republic of Congo. During his tenure, Bralima became one of the fastest growing businesses within Heineken. Dolf began his career at the Heineken Group Head Office in 1998 as a commercial management trainee.

Between 1999 and 2003, he occupied various marketing and sales roles within the Netherlands and for Heineken International. A native of The Netherlands, Dolf graduated from the University of Groningen with a dual master's degree in Business Administration and Philosophy.

In 2012, Fortune Magazine listed him as one of their "40 Under 40". He is a member of the 2014 Class of Henry Crown Fellows at the Aspen Institute.

Steve. J. Wilson

Until June 2005, Steve was President of Diageo's Reserve Brands Group responsible for the creation and development of the High end Spirits business which included Johnnie Walker Blue and Gold, Ciroc vodka ,Tanqueray 10 and Don Julio Tequila. Over a period of two years this business was expanded into 22 Countries.

Prior to this appointment, Steve headed up Innovation globally for Diageo and over the years has been associated with the creation of a number of major successes including Baileys Irish Cream, Bombay Sapphire, Archers Peach County Schnapps, Smirnoff Black, Malibu and more recently Smirnoff Ice and the Singleton single malt whisky.

He also specialises in developing new business ventures and brands in emerging markets including India, China, Brazil, Venezuela, Thailand and Africa.

With 38 years experience in new business development and innovation, he has held a number of other roles in Production management, Quality Control, Research and Development, Marketing and General Management.

In April 2005 he set up Invigor8tion Ltd, his own Marketing and Innovation consultancy and is working with a number of International organisations globally specialising in innovation best practise, coaching organisations and individuals in world class innovation as well as brand and business trouble shooting. Also, he continues to practise with the creation of premium brands, brand activation and experiential marketing and in developing businesses and brands in developing markets with successes in China, India, Thailand and Korea.

Steve also holds two non Executive Director Positions. McKinney Rogers Group Ltd, a management consulting company specialising in strategy to action and a Venture capital business. Also, The Informer where he works on drinks brands troubleshooting and experiential marketing.

In his spare time he restores and collects classic cars.

Index

About the Author

After a fast-track career with the UK Royal Marine Commandos, where he served for 18 years on operations around the world, Damian McKinney entered the private sector. He soon discovered that the Royal Marines' approach to challenging and complex military operations was directly relatable and transferable to the business world.

In 1999, he founded the company McKinney Rogers around his love of "real operational challenges", particularly under severe pressure and focusing on results. And over the past decade, he has built a global organization with offices on every subcontinent, and dedicated to delivering tangible and sustainable results for organizations ranging from Walmart to Diageo and Pfizer to Thomson Reuters.

McKinney Rogers applies military philosophy and real-world experience to equip business teams and organisations with the tools and capability to deliver high-performance results regardless of the obstacles they face

http://www.mckinneyrogers.com/